DATE DUE

GAYLORD   PRINTED IN U.S.A.

Raymond Lecoq

Classic French Wrought Iron

Foreword by Richard J. Wattenmaker

Translated by Gregory P. Bruhn

W. W. Norton & Company

New York • London

In the chapter on keys (page 117–125), museum and collector names are abbreviated:

Ca: Musée Calvet, Avignon.
Cl: Musée de Cluny, Paris.
Be: Bergue.
Fo: Fontaine.
Fr: Frank.
Mo: Montmelier.
Ve: Verdier.

Keys with no atttribution belong to the Musée Le Secq des Tournelles in Rouen.

Copyright © Societé d'Editions Littéraires et Documentaires, Paris, 1999.
English translation copyright © 2005 by W. W. Norton & Company, Inc.

Originally published in French as FER FORGÉ ET SERRURERIE

All rights reserved
Printed in the United States of America

For information about permission to reproduce selections from this book, write to
Permissions, W. W. Norton & Company, Inc., 500 Fifth Avenue, New York, NY 10110

Technical consultant: Jonathan Nedbor
Composition by Ken Gross
Manufacturing by Quebecor World Kingsport Press
Production manager: Leeann Graham

Library of Congress Cataloging-in-Publication Data

Lecoq, Raymond, 1913–1971.
    [Fer forgé et serrurerie. English]
    Classic French wrought iron / Raymond Lecoq ; preface by Richard J.
    Wattenmaker ; translated by Gregory P. Bruhn.
        p.   cm.
    Includes bibliographical references.
    ISBN 0-393-73157-X
       1 Architectural ironwork—France. 2. Wrought-iron—France. I. Title.
NA3950.L413 2004
2004056807

W. W. Norton & Company, Inc., 500 Fifth Avenue, New York, N.Y. 10110
www.wwnorton.com
W. W. Norton & Company Ltd., Castle House, 75/76 Wells St., London W1T 3QT

0 9 8 7 6 5 4 3 2 1

Contents

Foreword

My wife and I met Raymond Lecoq (1913–1971) in the spring of 1970. We were introduced to him by the legendary connoisseur Michel Meyer, whose picturesque Dickensian shop on the rue du Four, around the corner from the rue du Dragon, where so many American art students in years past had studied at the Académie Julian, was an obligatory stop on the pilgrimage route of devoted collectors of old ironwork. At the time, Lecoq was completing what were to become his last books: *Serrurerie Ancienne, techniques et oeuvres* (1973) and *Les Objets de la vie domestique* (1979). The latter was of special interest to us as it dealt with what was the primary focus of our fledgling collection. Lecoq and his wife, Micheline, the scholar's highly knowledgeable aide in his investigations, took us foreigners in tow and introduced us into the circle of French iron prospectors. Lecoq was generous and forthright, sharing his comprehensive experience and wide-ranging contacts.

Lecoq invited us to join him on his regular Saturday route through the flea markets at Saint-Ouen, where we observed the method by which he had discriminatingly assembled an extensive collection that doubled as a point of reference for his research. He would examine tools that dealers offered as merely "old" and, knowing both their purpose and age, would casually pay two francs or a bit more to obtain a rarity. He had known many of these merchants for years, and as he exchanged pleasantries with them, they punctuated their banter with a drumbeat of questions, all of which he tactfully answered. When urged to confirm a date earlier than what he felt was justified by the evidence, his response would invariably be a laconic "perhaps" that adroitly yet amicably punctured the merchant's eternally inflated hopes. He also took us to the annual *Foire à la ferraille et au jambon* (literally, "the fair of scrap iron and ham," the origin of which reached back to the Middle Ages) at la Villette (the location, until modern times, of the abattoirs of Paris). He invited us to see a demonstration of the blacksmith's craft chez Bataillard on the rue Lepic, where we met the patriarch of the firm, then over ninety, who vividly recounted episodes from his life before the turn of the century when daily he rode a bicycle from St.-Germain-en-Laye to Montmartre and often saw Toulouse-Lautrec (d. 1901) in the quarter. I asked if he had served in World War I. With gentle indignation, recalling an unpleasant memory, he replied, "I was too old for the war. I had already spent three years in the army in the 90s," adding for emphasis, "day by day!"

Lecoq accompanied us to dealers in Paris such as the incomparable Jean Monin, then occupying a large gallery on the Boulevard Clichy where one could always buy high-quality objects at reasonable prices. He introduced us to collectors, men assiduous in their individual approaches to the passion they shared and friendly to a curious newcomer. One day, Lecoq suggested we meet so that I might accompany him to visit Mr. Hotermans, a collector who maintained an apartment near the Parc Monceau solely to house his enormous—approximately two thousand pieces—collection of ironwork. The accumulation, spread out among five or six rooms, contained multiple examples that Lecoq used as the basis for many of his drawings and photographs, which traced the typological evolution of certain utensils. Although the actual building had long since disappeared, each time I arrived at Lecoq's home on the rue Clauzel for our rendezvous, I could never dismiss from my mind that this was the very location of *père*

Julien Tanguy's shop, where, in the 1870s and 1880s, the impressionist artists bought their painting supplies. It also was virtually the only place where Cézanne's work could be seen and purchased. Hotermans, whose collection found a home in the David M. Stewart Museum in Montreal not long after my visit, was an odd type who evidently thought I was a potential purchaser, particularly for his irregularly shaped and self-framed nonobjective paintings that distantly resembled late Kandinsky. While he rambled on about the pictures, I studied the ironwork, with which some years later I was to have a reunion in Canada when my wife and I organized a modest exhibition in 1975 that toured museums throughout the province of Ontario.

Lecoq had a galvanic effect on our approach toward wrought iron. When I told him of our journeys throughout regions of France where early medieval iron is abundant and in situ, notably in Auvergne and Roussillon, and showed him photographs we had taken of hinges, locks, door pulls, and grillework, he, an expert photographer and classifier of Cartesian proclivities, scolded me for not having recorded their exact dimensions. He provided us with the names and locations of antiques and secondhand dealers throughout France where we might find objects for modest prices. Long before, he had set himself the task of systematically walking the streets of every city he visited in order to photograph its ironwork—grilles, balconies, stair railings, door knockers, hinges, and the like. The result of this work was an extensive personal archive of more than 9,000 images that supplemented his comprehensive and intimate knowledge of often obscure written sources. Lecoq's research thus builds on and extends the tradition of such nineteenth- and early twentieth-century French scholars such as Liger, Havard, Frémont, Blanc, Husson, and d'Allemagne.

On a chilly early spring morning the three of us traveled to Rouen, where we really saw Lecoq in action *sur le motif.* The reserves of the Le Secq des Tournelles Museum were opened and Lecoq, deftly maneuvering his Rolleiflex to obtain the optimum lighting, recorded images that were destined to serve as illustrations in his books. That day he was working on kitchen utensils, our favorite subject. It was a unique treat to explore the collections at leisure, for although I had first visited that unequalled assemblage six years earlier, nothing could compare to seeing the choicest of objects through Lecoq's eyes and actually holding them in our hands. We had a pleasant surprise when Catherine Vaudour, curator of the museum and later herself the author of valuable publications on ironwork, approached Lecoq to ask if he would give an impromptu demonstration to a group of visiting students who were from a technical high school in Germany and wished to learn about the workings of intricate seventeenth-century locks. Lecoq set about his task by carefully surveying the vitrines and decisively selecting an example with the most elaborate mechanism with which to make his points. With the youngsters' instructor translating, he held the students in rapt attention as he revealed the secrets of the highly complex internal workings of a masterpiece lock. As we were no less students than the teenagers, we were fascinated and privileged to see such a born teacher at work. Later we paid a visit to the Musée Départemental des Antiquités de la Seine-Maritime and concluded the memorable day with a tour of the churches of St. Ouen, St. Maclou, and the cathedral immortalized by Monet, as well as several out-of-the-way antique shops without which the trip would not have been complete.

As an American, I was not the first by any means to fall under the spell of French ironwork. Edgar B. Frank, George Gray Barnard, Elie Nadelman, Samuel Yellin, Albert C. Barnes, and Dominique de Menil were among my more illustrious predecessors. Indeed, many French thought Frank a native, but I had read his book, *Old French Ironwork,* published by Harvard University Press in 1950, two years after it had appeared in French as *Petite Ferronnerie Ancienne* (Editions Self, 1948) and knew that he was an expatriate living in France since 1910, when he had come over to represent an American hardware firm. A sophisticated collector and contemporary of Henri Le Secq and Henry-René d'Allemagne, Frank later recounted some of his experiences with French dealers in a little-known memoir titled *La Brocante sentimental* (Nouvelles Editions Latines, 1950). In addition to admiring Frank's work, which Lecoq described in the bibliography of the present volume as having been "presented with love and competence," Lecoq also highly valued the *Made of Iron* catalog for the 1966 exhibition in Houston, organized by the great French expatriate collector Dominique de Menil, who had unique access to private collectors, dealers, and museums that enabled her to borrow some of the rarest objects for her show from such discerning collectors as Meyer and Nicolas Landau.

Lecoq not only led us to sources, including antiquarian book dealers, but often accompanied us to see what we, on a strictly limited budget, had chosen to purchase, and he gave us the benefit of his wisdom and experience. He was straightforward and undogmatic in spirit and tenacious in the chase, and we were able to communicate even though my French language skills and accent were a definite strain on his ears. We would search through Paris and subsequently meet to show or describe to him what we had seen or found. I remember our satisfaction in seeing Lecoq himself acquire objects we had come across in some obscure boutique but had passed over due to our self-imposed financial restraints. I think it amused him to see how much ground we covered. In the course of our conversations, I inquired about some of the beautiful objects in his collection and he related how he scored a coup at the Hôtel Drouot during the 1968 demonstrations when people were afraid to go out into the streets and Lecoq was the sole bidder at the scheduled auction.

Raymond Lecoq never lived to see his final tomes published or to fulfill his long-range research projects. *Classic French Wrought Iron* has special meaning for me. As we were departing Paris on, as it turned out, the last day I ever saw him, he presented me with a copy of this book, inscribed: "To Richard Wattenmaker, hoping that this study will render him service in order to classify his finds. Warmly. Paris May 31, 1970." Together with his other writings, it has. The gentle intensity, conviction of purpose, and insight with which Raymond Lecoq's investigations were infused resulted in solid achievements that continue to enrich the fund of knowledge for students and scholars alike. I am therefore honored to contribute this brief reminiscence to the English-language edition of this important study.

Richard J. Wattenmaker
Director, Archives of American Art
Smithsonian Institution
Washington, D.C.

From grilles to pipe cleaners—without overlooking anything that involves protection, security, furnishings, heating, lighting, jewelry and other finery—rare are the themes that don't inspire ironsmiths and locksmiths.

The range of decorative possibilities requires a unique response to each demand, as much in terms of dimension or execution as decoration. Whether forging a railing or a piece of jewelry, ironworkers always work logically, while allowing the iron to maintain its character. In those rare attempts at imitating another technique (as can been seen, for example, at the Louvre where a small grate of Spanish origin was executed as an *orbe-voie* [a relief effect achieved by superimposing sheets of pierced metal] and has the appearance of carved woodwork), the metalsmith can highlight either the subtlety or robustness of the working material.

Ironworkers do not disregard anything: All scrolling and leafwork is done with careful attention, in the same way as the finishing of a key.

In order to simplify the research in this vast domain, it seemed necessary, on the one hand, to study the technical issues by analyzing the different factors that one is required to keep in mind in order to create a work of iron, and, on the other hand, to create tables that synthesize the evolution of forms across each style. We also wanted to illustrate our presentation with numerous examples. We chose works that are generally unknown and then added other, more typical works, examples that couldn't be left out.

Defining the characteristics of a style or era with a small number of schematic diagrams seemes like a gamble. The *Tour de France des Compagnons Serruriers* has tended to unify style and technique, but each region still leaves an imprint on its works, which also reflects the personal touch of each fabricator and at times a faithfulness to older techniques or the innovation of others. In addition, most external grillework has to be restored over time and the repoussé leafing completely renewed. These restorations are more often faithful to the approach of the artisan-restorer than they are to the spirit of the work. It is also not uncommon to see elements of a forged grille from the thirteenth century mounted on a rolled-iron frame (see, for example, the grates from the Abbey of Saint-Denis or the Musée de Cluny) or Louis XVI leafwork on a Louis XIV grille.

Moreover, the great skill of certain modern master artisans at reproducing styles from the past often makes it difficult to differentiate between a period piece and a recent work.

We were able to witness the restoration of the grilles at Place Stanislas in Nancy. The ornamental repoussé foliate leaves eroded by rust had to be almost entirely redone. The principal metalsmith in charge of this work was so accurate in his interpretation and understanding that only a careful analysis could reveal the restored parts.

We have thought it worthwhile to analyze the evolution of technique and style with a few charts, despite the difficulties that such an inquiry entails.

We hope that readers will indulge us!

A Working Outline

Several variables, including final use, function, conditions of construction, and construction specifications affect the making of an ironwork project. The ironworker must complete the work in the simplest, most logical fashion, with the available technical means and allocated budget.

The outline below is not definitive; it is a working outline that may help to facilitate research based on conceptualization and construction.

1. Final use	Plan	Usage
		Usefulness
		Dimensions
2. Function	Security	Protection from collapse
		Protection against break-ins
		Protection against weather conditions
	Airtightness	Water
		Air
		Dust
		Noise
	Aesthetics	Composition
		Relationship of sizes
		Design, ornamentation
		Characteristics of the various styles
3. Conditions of construction	Solidness, rigidity	Expected demands (stresses)
		Possible deformations
		Choice of material
		Choice of assembly
	Economic considerations	Choice of profile (Standardization: A.F.NOR)
		Knowledge of machines and tools
		Analysis of production
	Permanence of the work	Protection of metallic work:
		• against corrosion caused by rain and condensation
		• against electrolytic conductivity

4. Construction specifications	A. Contacts	Removable	Screws, bolts, axles, pins, keys
		Permanent	Nails, rivets, collars, joints
		Soldered	Malleable: pewters Durable: brazing and soldering Welded: oxy-acetylene and electric
		Solid	Assemblage: 　Half-lap joint 　Tenon and mortise 　By penetration: rounded hole 　With pins 　Dovetail 　Angled bars 　Gusset-plates
		Flexible	Leaf spring Coil spring (spring hinges)
		Temporary	Lock parts
	B. Guides	Translatory	Sliding frame Horizontal and vertical
		Rotation	French-style openings
		Translatory rotation	Accordion doors Italian frame Canadian frame Australian frame
	C. Articulations		Pintles, strap hinges, pins, plates for door hinges

Nantes. Hôtel de Villestreux. 18th century. 3 place de la Petite Hollande

The Iron Industry

Textual indications, confirmed by archeological discovery, establish the importance of the steel industry in Celtic countries and notably in Gaul during the La Tène period (450 to about 58 B.C.E.). Numerous vestiges attest to the fact that, in the last century B.C.E., the Gauls knew how to reduce iron oxides. If they had not yet discovered smelting, which requires quite elevated temperatures (2,372–2,552°F), they were at least producing a high-quality iron steel.

Most often, a furnace—a simple cavity with walls of fire-resistant soil reinforced with crude stones—was hollowed out of a hillside. It contained a little more than 10 cubic meters (353 cubic feet) of crushed ores and charcoal in alternating horizontal layers. A hole in the base served as ventilation and collected bits of raw iron, which were purified and then refined by repeated hammering while still hot.

It took until the eleventh century for the art of ironwork to be reborn in France. Blacksmiths used charcoal to heat the ore, reducing the iron oxides to form a bloom of iron and steel. Forging and repeated welding slowly transformed the spongy mass into workable bars and plate. As a result of this process, the low carbon iron exhibits an exceptional suppleness, ductility, and durability. Large-scale wrought pieces were quite rare: they never exceeded 440 pounds or measured more than 4 meters (13 feet). Far from being an obstacle, this restriction allowed for a certain ironworking perfection to be obtained.

The first rolling mills and tilt-hammers, run by water power, were put to use in France at the end of the sixteenth century, under Henri II, and put ready-to-use iron at the blacksmith's disposal. From then on, and especially starting in the era of Louis XIII, work carried the mark of this technical evolution and lacked the charm of creations from the twelfth century, when the irregularity of the material added a touch of vitality to medieval compositions.

In the first half of the eighteenth century, the large ingot molds of cast iron became known as pigs. These came in the form of triangular prisms and weighed from 15 to 1,800 pounds, sometimes more. Once puddled, the pigs were beaten out with large hammers, and forged into bars about 1 meter (3 feet) in length.

The quality of the iron, whether rough or soft, was determined by examining the grain at its breaking point. Iron from the Lorraine region was reputed the softest. Those from the Berry and Nevers regions and from along the banks of the Loire held second place. Iron from Burgundy was classed as rock, half-rock, and common irons. After forming, the smallest iron pieces of 4 to 5 lines (a line being a twelfth of an inch, or approximately 21.2 centimeters) were called *chimes*. All of the other pieces, varying from 9 lines to 26 square centimeters (4 square inches), were known by the designation *square irons*.

The modern steel industry offers metalsmiths quite an extensive choice of iron sizes. But metal obtained from fusion using hydroelectric power (even today's soft irons) does not possess the same degree of quality in suppleness and ductility that charcoal treatment gave it.

The naming of commercial iron varies according to its size. For dimensions, which are standardized, one can consult the French standards published by A.F.NOR (Assocation Française de Normalisation).

Square iron (fig. 1) is called a *billet* when the side is 35 to 110 millimeters (1.4 to 4.3 inches) long, and *bloom* when the side is 115 to 300 millimeters (4.5 to 11.7 inches) long.

Rectangular irons (fig. 2) are called *flat* when the width is 200 to 300 millimeters (7.8 to 11.7 inches) and the thickness is 7 to 40 millimeters (3 to 1.6 inches), *slab* when the width is 115 to 300 millimeters (4.5 to 11.7 inches) and the thickness is 65 to 250 millimeters (2.5 to 9.75 inches), and *rough-hewn* when the width is 55 to 145 millimeters (2.1 to 5.7 inches) and the thickness is 45 to 70 millimeters (1.8 to 2.7 inches).

The current designations are as follows: half-flat (fig. 3), flat (fig. 4), strip (fig. 5), square (fig. 6), round (fig. 7), half-round (fig. 8), hexagonal (fig. 9), octagonal (fig. 10), round tube (fig. 11), square tube (fig. 12), rectangular tube (fig. 13), and hollow half-round (fig. 14).

For metal construction and framework, the designations are as follows: angle-irons with equal or unequal leg angles, open or closed (fig. 15), T-beams (fig. 16), U-beams, regular or sharp angle (fig. 17), I-beams (fig. 18), and wide or thin slots (fig. 19).

A whole range of special forms, whose juxtaposition allows you to achieve numerous arrangements, is used in structural steel (fig. 20).

The use of these irons makes the artisan's work easier, but they can give a cold or impersonal touch to the production, especially if the conveniences afforded by current available techniques are overused. Hence the abundance of distressed iron sold under the name *wrought iron*.

A few iron artisans, however, continue to work according to tradition. They often convert square iron into rectangular iron, giving the lifeless, manufactured mass a life and vibrancy that only intense forging can produce. They do not proceed by removal of the material, avoiding the file and grindstone. Instead they use iron's plastic quality to give form to the metal.

Blacksmiths prefer forge or hammer welding and only very sparingly use modern processes. Their works thereby acquire personal qualities that other works executed in rolled iron can not achieve.

Cross Sections in Current Use

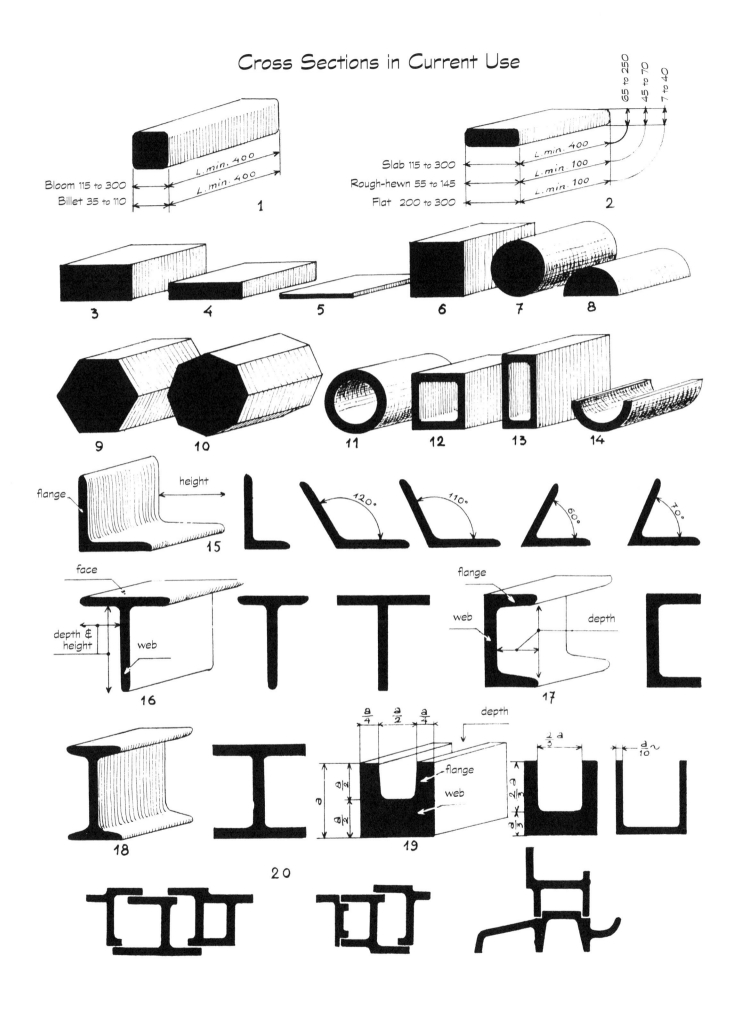

Bloom 115 to 300
Billet 35 to 110
L.min. 400
L.min. 400
1

65 to 250
45 to 70
7 to 40
Slab 115 to 300
Rough-hewn 55 to 145
Flat 200 to 300
L.min. 400
L.min. 100
L.min. 100
2

3 4 5 6 7 8

9 10 11 12 13 14

flange height
15

120° 110° 60° 70°

face
depth & height web
16

flange web depth
17

18

$\frac{a}{4}$ $\frac{a}{2}$ $\frac{a}{4}$ depth $\frac{2a}{3}$ $\frac{d}{10}\sim$
a $\frac{a}{2}$ flange $\frac{2a}{3}$
$\frac{a}{2}$ web $\frac{a}{3}$
19

20

Assembly

By accentuating the technical details, the ironworker emphasizes structure and gives more force to his or her compositions.

In an ironwork design, contact points are to be avoided as much as possible, as they create an optical illusion in which thicker parts appear to stick out. To de-emphasize these thick contact points, the ironworker can either reinforce them using a ring within the frame or with a rivet against the frame, or eliminate them altogether using an intermediary ball.

Assembly designs are often quite diverse; we will therefore only cite the major ones:

1. Ring, collar, tie, or tieback. Assembly pieces used to hold together several overlapping ironwork elements; in general, the collar is closed around the work hot, without welding. Employing these elements greatly enriches the composition of the work.

2. Swelled or pass-through joint. Bars are inserted through the crosspiece. This type of construction does not weaken the metal's resistance as do half-lap joints. Moreover, it accentuates the technical requirements while creating a play between shadow and light. The dimension of the bar (C) determines the external dimension of the bulging joint (2C). Square bar, flush (fig. 2), square bar, angled (fig. 3), round bar (fig. 4).

5. Rivet with visible head. Here, again, the assembly style is accentuated.

6. Rivet with flush head. To be avoided when possible.

7. Riveted intermediary ball. The contact point is avoided and the composition appears more open.

8. Screw. Allows for easy disassembly (side view).

9. Screw assembly.

10. Mortise and tenon, riveted.

11. Mortise and tenon.

12. Half-lap joint, on the end, held together by a rivet.

13. Dowel, pinned.

14. Rivet, pinned.

15. Half-lap joint, used in the interior of a design, ensures an overall solidness.

16. Connection pin, brazed in the post, fixed in the crosspiece. To ensure better assembly, the hole bored into the crosspiece for the linchpin should not line up with the hole in the dowel. In this way, the crosspiece is brought back and jammed into the post.

17. Dovetail. This prevents transverse slippage and tearing.

18. Dowel, riveted or soldered. This type of assembly is mostly used for attaching leafwork. It forms a continuous line with the iron, without any protuberance.

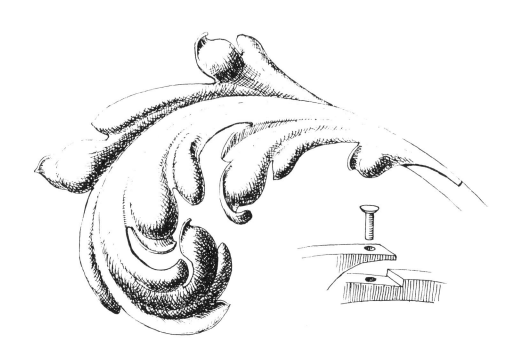

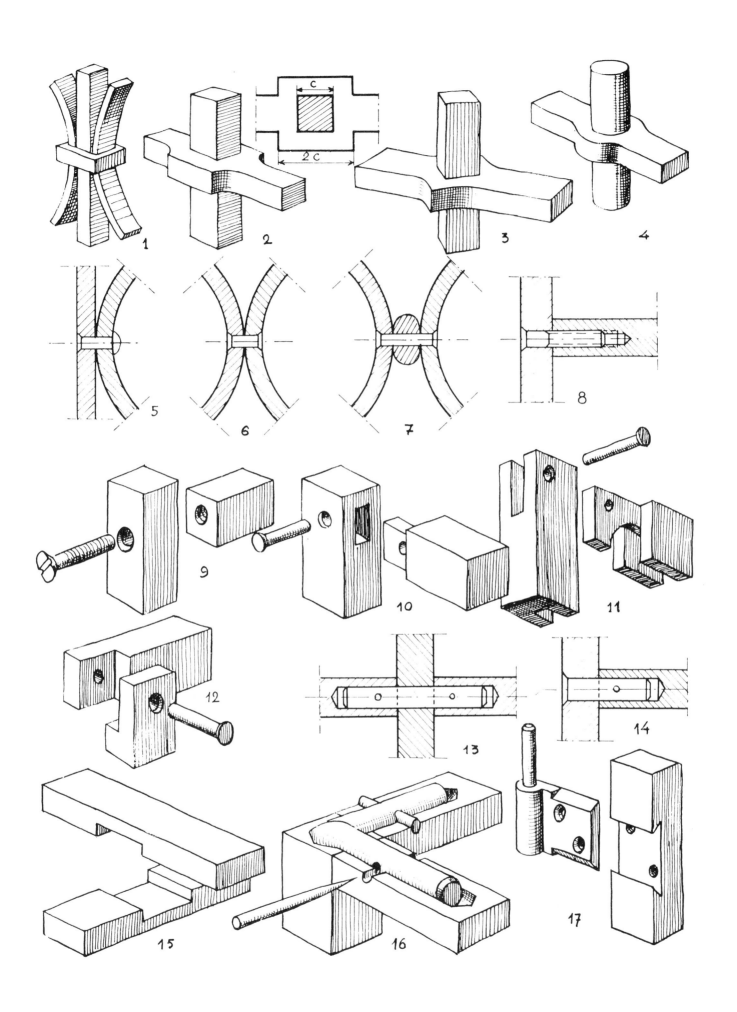

Forge Techniques

A single person can generally execute most forge work. Several operations, however, require the participation of an assistant, or striker. The ironsmith responsible for the work holds the metal in his left hand and, with the right, guides or hits with the striking tool. The assistant hits with the face of the hammer, which he grips with two hands. A tool fixed into the eye of the anvil can complement the striking tool, in order to accomplish two tasks at once. The gorge and the tool placed in the anvil hole to form a groove are an example.

The top of the anvil has three distinct work areas: a rectangular *face*, and at either end are the round *horn* and square horn, or *heel*.

The type of hammer used by the smith differs greatly from that of the woodworker. It has two faces, generally a flat face for forging and a narrow face best suited to spreading the metal.

Following are definitions of professional terms that readers should know in order to understand ironsmithing and its evolution. In the corresponding drawings, which illustrate forging techniques, the hot metal parts are shaded.

Bending: Executed on the round horn or over the far edge of the anvil to create curves or angles.

Corner bends: The iron, held in a vise, is bent and formed with a hammer.

Fullering: Grooves are created on one or both sides of the iron with the help of a top fuller alone, or in conjunction with a bottom fuller.

Shouldering: The shoulder, started with a fuller, is drawn out and the step is sharpened with a *set hammer* (1) and the area dressed with a *flatter* (2). Generally, iron is shouldered on one side for half-lap assembly (fig. 1), and on both sides to create a tenon (fig. 2).

Punching: An operation that creates a hole, causing the surrounding area to bulge outward. The punch may have a circular, elliptical, square, or rectangular cross section.

Slitting: To cut lengthwise with the help of a hot-set or chisel. The tool in the illustrated example is a hot-set.

Cutting: A hot-cut is used from above or a hardie from below. The hot-cut and hardie can be used together, one above the other.

Upsetting: The metal is heated in the spot where a bulge is desired, then struck on the end.

Swaging: The heated metal is roughed out with the hammer and then placed between the top and bottom swages. The top swage is then struck with a sledge. The hot metal inside will be formed by and take the shape and size of the swage.

Curving: Execution of curved forms on the horn or beak iron. The horn's conical shape creates, from the base to the tip, smaller and smaller circles. The smith works on the part of the circle that is closest to the desired curve.

Drawing out: The heated metal is stretched with a hammer. The illustration shows a taper being drawn out.

Flattening: Using a *flatter*, with its large flat face, will remove the surface irregularities from hammering.

Hammer or forge welding: Two pieces of metal, at a sweating heat, are welded by hammering them together on the anvil. Because the iron is reduced in size by this hammering, it is necessary to allow for a surplus of metal in the area to be welded, by *upsetting*:

1. Lap or scarf weld
2. Cleft weld
3. Butt weld

Twisting: The iron is held in a vise; a round tube the length of the desired twist—with a diameter equal to the square or rectangular cross section of the iron—is slid over the metal. With the help of a wrench, the metal is turned as much as is necessary. It is unnecessary to heat stock of 1/2 inch in cross section or less.

Scroll forming: The end of the scroll is created with a hammer, then, with the help of a clamp or *bending fork*, the hot metal is bent against the scroll form. This type of execution is used when the smith needs to create several scrolls of the same form.

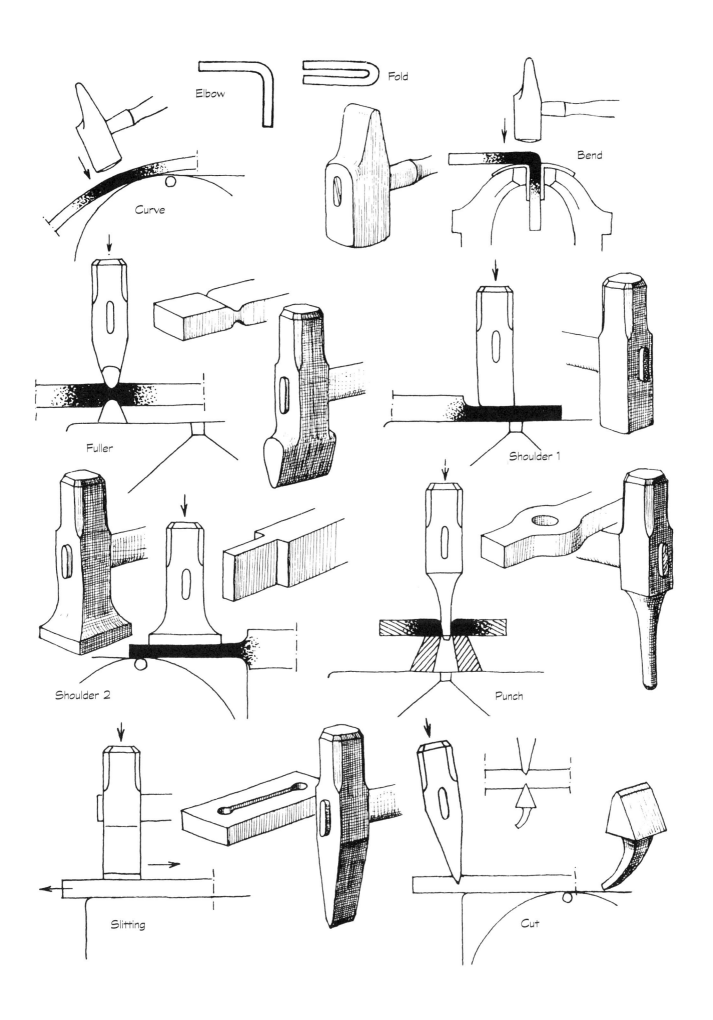

Elbow

Fold

Curve

Bend

Fuller

Shoulder 1

Shoulder 2

Punch

Slitting

Cut

15

It is worth giving an overview of the main technical procedures and means that through the ages allowed ironsmiths to express themselves while respecting the limits of the material.

Brazing

Though dating far back in time, brazing wasn't commonly used until the seventeenth century. In order to braze, a piece of more fusible metal (usually copper) and a flux (borax) are heated until the brazing material has melted between the two iron surfaces.

Collars

Quite common in the Middle Ages, this type of assembly was abandoned in the eighteenth century. Its cross section tended to be rectangular in the eleventh century, then in a half-round in the thirteenth (the strap-hinge tiebacks were swaged). Seldom used in the fourteenth and fifteenth centuries, it acquired, at the end of the sixteenth and through the seventeenth centuries, a particular molded cross section (a half-circle laid onto a rectangle) called a *half-round moulding*, which was sometimes decorated with a floral motif.

Damasquine (à la damasquine)

In use during the Renaissance, this type of engraving cut costs and left the design in relief.

Damascening (damascened)

This is an inlay of gold, silver, or even copper on iron, common on sixteenth-century arms and armor. The design is engraved so that the bottom of the groove is undercut (wider), creating a dovetail shaped channel. The inlay metal, fashioned into a wire, is set in the channel and hammered to spread it down into the undercut areas, thus securing it.

Stamping

An ancestor of modern die work, this process, used from the end of the twelfth century and common in the thirteenth century, still played a role in the seventeenth century in the creation of half-round moulding and flower pistils. A sample piece is made, to be used as a positive in making an impression in a hot blank. The resulting die or swage allows for quick reproduction of a specific form. The iron is beaten into the negative of the die and trimmed if necessary. A two-sided form requires a set of top and bottom dies. In the seventeenth and eighteenth centuries many structural shapes were done with dies or swages. Most English keys of this period were cold stamped in dies using a press.

Chasing

Used mostly during the Renaissance, it was still employed during the seventeenth and eighteenth centuries for decorating master locks. The technique consists of using a chisel to impress the lines of a design into the surface of the metal. It is also used to impart a sharper outline to hollow elements formed with a hammer or repoussé.

Piercing (often called *orbe-voie* or *double-fond*)

Appearing as early as the fourteenth century and still in use in the middle of the sixteenth century for decorating locks, this technique was also used in Spain for decorating grillework.

A thin piece of sheet metal was sawn or chiseled along the lines of a certain layout or design; on this sheet metal was placed another piece of sheet metal that had wider holes (sometimes a third, also pierced, was added to the two prior plates). The relief impression created by the layering was further accentuated for locks and metal fittings by a leather or red fabric backing. The second plate was sometimes replaced by molded iron rods, which highlighted the relief even more.

Repoussé

In use in the sixteenth century for decorating locks, bolts, and knockers, repoussé made its way into the creation of foliage in the seventeenth and eighteenth centuries. It can be executed in several ways:

1. A sheet of metal is pushed into a metal die or mold, using various hammers and chisels. This work is quite close to swaging, except that repoussé ornamentation is hollow, whereas swaged ornamentation is solid.
2. A thin metal sheet is applied to a wood core, as in goldwork.
3. Applied to the back side of the work, which is mounted on pitch (a semi-hard base of asphaltum, oil, and resin), the thin metal is pushed with small chisels and punches, which form the desired relief. Then the piece is turned over and worked on the face in the same manner to sharpen the design.
4. The foliage is stamped onto little bits of thin sheet metal of different shapes, with the help of various hammers. The stamping is done on the underside of the sheet metal to raise the forms and then on the front to sharpen the relief.

Riveting

Dating back to the La Tène era, the rivet reappeared at the end of the twelfth century. Used for joining two or more pieces of metal, it is an iron pin with a head at one end. The rivet is inserted, hot or cold, into a hole through the layers of metal to be joined, and the plain end is flared with a hammer to form a head. When done hot, the rivet contracts as it cools. The head may be decorated and would be set with a rivet snap, giving the head its finished shape.

Forge or hammer welding

The original welding technique, using the hammer to join two pieces of iron at a sweating or white heat, is still the preferred method for many smiths, though the characteristics of some modern alloys do not readily lend themselves to this process.

Screw

As a way to secure parts, the screw, which appeared at the end of the fifteenth century, didn't enter into common usage until a century later. Let's not forget, along these lines, the threading lathe, among the numerous inventions that we owe to Leonardo da Vinci.

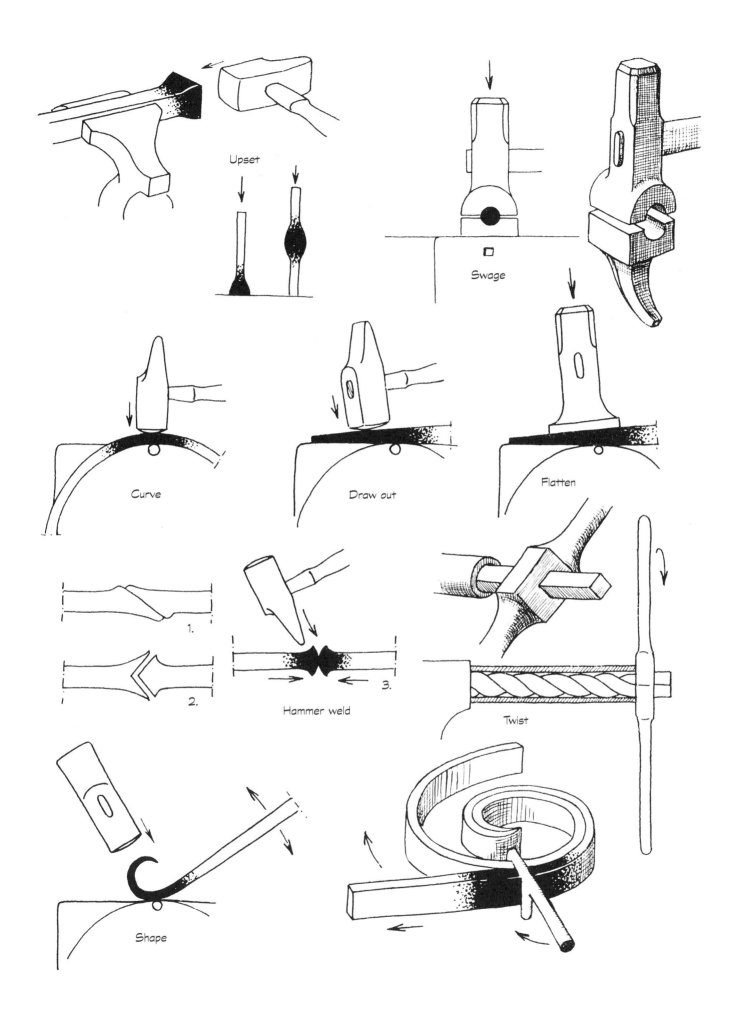

Upset

Swage

Curve

Draw out

Flatten

1.

2.

Hammer weld

3.

Twist

Shape

Aesthetics

If there is no single process for creating a work of art, there are at least a few fundamental principles that can facilitate its elaboration. The main laws that govern ornamentation apply equally to ironwork composition, and the ironsmith's preoccupations, as well the decorator's, can be summarized as:

Why, where, how?

This is to say that function, placement, and space demand artistic research. An exterior protective grille, for example, is not conceived of in the same manner as a purely ornamental interior grille: The former must prevent people and animals from entering while still letting in light; the latter erects a mere mental barrier. A decor that is heavier in design in its lower sections may perform double duty, expressing a utilitarian sturdiness and simultaneously preventing animals from entering. Less heavily loaded at eye level, the design lightens the composition's overall appearance and allows light to pass through.

The dimensions of a piece of ironwork generally depend on its use, as a door or window for example, and it is practically impossible to modify them.

It goes without saying that placement affects the design. Once the design has found its rightful location, its execution will be more meticulous and the form more refined, as the eye is better able to pick out the work's details. Early ironsmiths understood this well, putting more finishing touches on ground-floor and lower-floor balconies than on those of upper floors.

As for the means, we will simply note that they are determined on the one hand by available funds and on the other by available tools and materials.

After acknowledging these three points, the ironsmith must decide on a viable decorative choice. Avoiding irregular shapes, the smith tends to highlight the square, rectangle, circle, and ellipse.

In addition, the division of the vertical rectangle on a grille can follow one of the following thirteen formulas:

1. Through simple repetition, even networks. An option used in the twelfth and thirteenth centuries and taken up again more recently.
2. Through simple repetition, alternating networks. A little-used decorative style; there are, however, a few examples from the fourteenth century.
3. Symmetrical on a vertical axis. This is the classic composition *par excellence*, seventeenth and eighteenth century.
4. Symmetrical with two axes, one vertical and one horizontal.
5. In vertical bands. Not a widely used composition.
6. Simple repetition with friezes. A decorative option used in the thirteenth century and the beginning of the seventeenth century.
7. Bars with lower panels. Classical composition.
8. Bars, lower panels, and transoms. Classical composition, seventeenth and eighteenth centuries.
9. Bars with friezes. Classical composition.
10. Bars with framework. Louis XVI and Empire eras.
11. In horizontal bands. Used mostly in the sixteenth and beginning of the seventeenth centuries.
12. In regular panels. A more contemporary option.
13. Asymmetrical. Characteristic of Louis XV style.

For a horizontal rectangle, balcony, or radiator cover, for example, the following ornamentation was adopted:

1. Simple repetition. Characteristic of the beginning of the seventeenth century, reappears under Louis XVI.
2. Simple repetition with frieze. A theme used in the seventeenth century.
3. In horizontal bands. A formula not widely used.
4. Symmetrical on a vertical axis. Classical composition.
5. Symmetrical on two axes. Louis XIV style.
6. Asymmetrical. Louis XV style.
7. Irregular panels. Louis XIV style.
8. Regular panels.
9. Panels and pilasters. End of the seventeenth and eighteenth century.

The ironsmith must focus on highlighting technical requirements instead of hiding them. By accentuating the method of assembly, the smith avoids an indecisive design look that arises from tangential curves. Adding a collar, which was a common procedure in the Middle Ages and under Louis XIII, is a way of doing this and further reviving thinner sections. In the same way, the use of small decorative balls, which started in the eighteenth century, lightens up the composition by avoiding points of contact. It is equally possible to create and assemble half-lap joints, a technique that began with Louis XIV.

When curved sections intersect and cross, it is preferable to overlay the bars so that the junction exhibits a look of fullness.

Decorative Partitions

1. Simple repetitions.
   Even network.
   Pages 58, 59, 60, 66, 67.

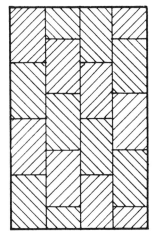

2. Simple repetitions.
   Alternating network.
   Pages 63, 64.

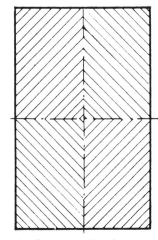

3. Symmetrical on a
   vertical axis.
   Pages 71, 74, 78.

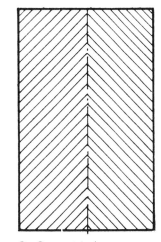

4. Symmetrical with two
   axes.
   Page 69.

5. Vertical bands.
   Pages 58, 59, 61.

6. Simple repetition with
   friezes.
   Pages 62, 71.

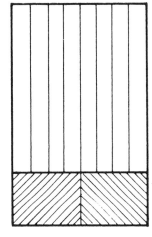

7. Bars with lower panels.
   Page 79.

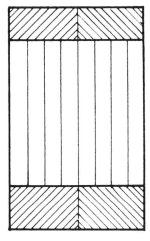

8. Bars, lower panels, and
   transoms.
   Page 73.

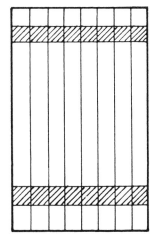

9. Bars and friezes.
   Pages 65, 68, 70.

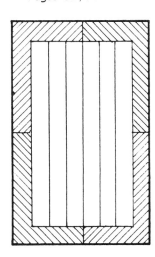

10. Bars and framework.
    Pages 76, 77.

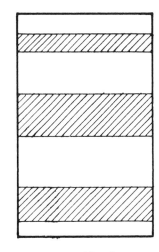

11. Horizontal bands.
    Pages 66, 70.

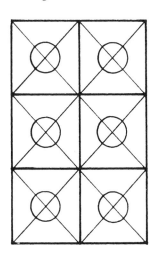

12. Regular panels.
    Page 71.

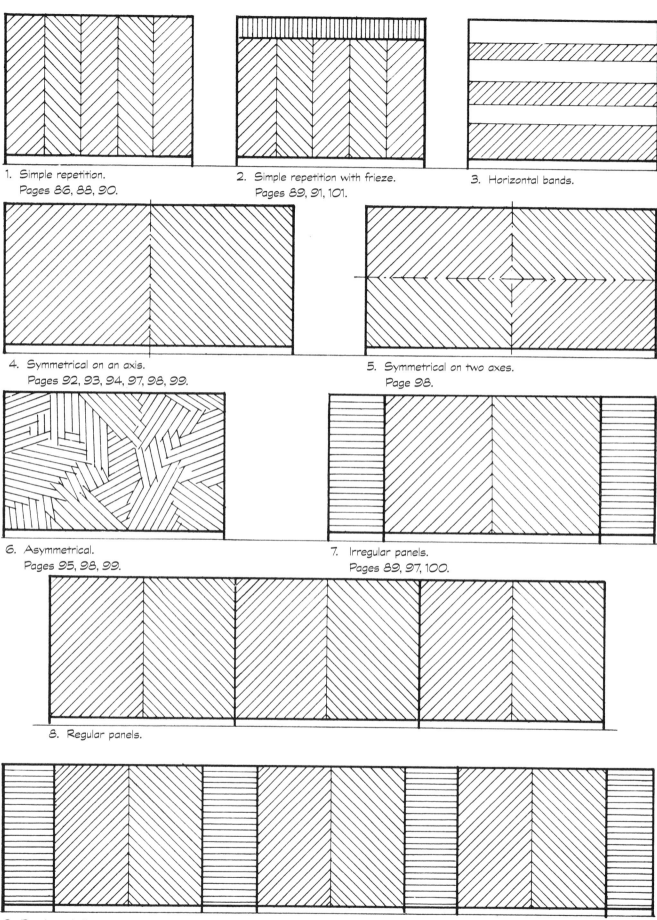

1. Simple repetition.
   Pages 86, 88, 90.

2. Simple repetition with frieze.
   Pages 89, 91, 101.

3. Horizontal bands.

4. Symmetrical on an axis.
   Pages 92, 93, 94, 97, 98, 99.

5. Symmetrical on two axes.
   Page 98.

6. Asymmetrical.
   Pages 95, 98, 99.

7. Irregular panels.
   Pages 89, 97, 100.

8. Regular panels.

9. Panels and pilasters.
   Page 93.

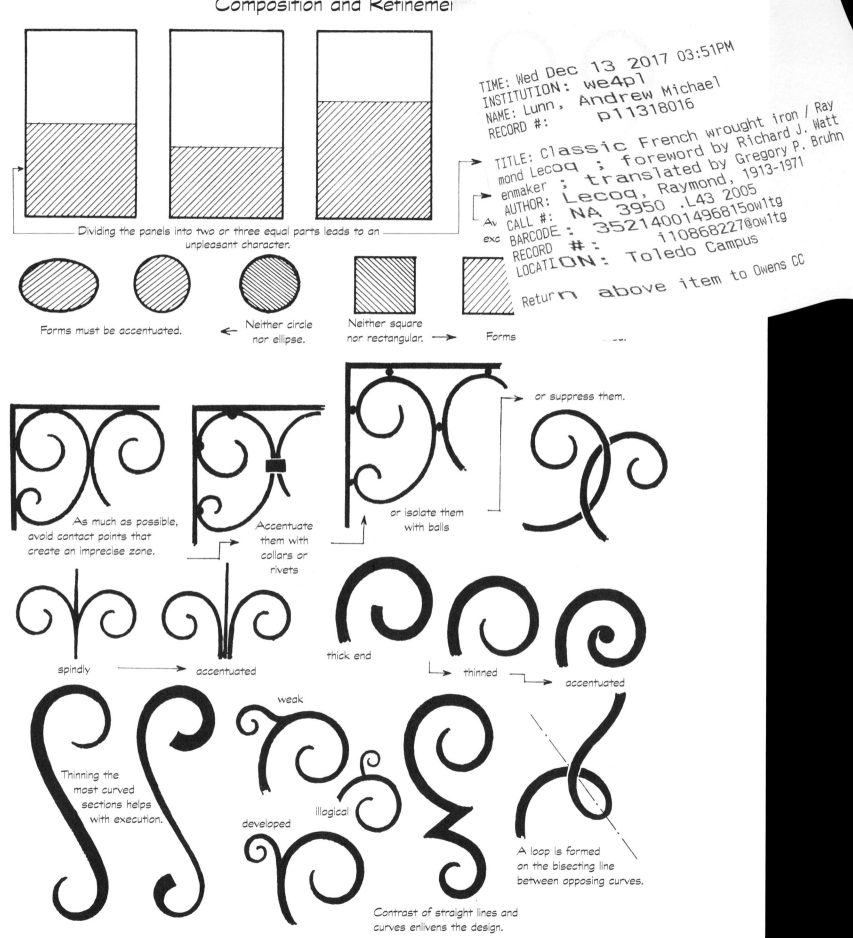

Dividing the panels into two or three equal parts leads to an unpleasant character.

Forms must be accentuated.

← Neither circle nor ellipse.

Neither square nor rectangular. →

Forms

or suppress them.

As much as possible, avoid contact points that create an imprecise zone.

Accentuate them with collars or rivets

or isolate them with balls

spindly → accentuated

thick end → thinned → accentuated

weak

Thinning the most curved sections helps with execution.

developed

illogical

A loop is formed on the bisecting line between opposing curves.

Contrast of straight lines and curves enlivens the design.

A locksmith's workshop in the 16th century, from a print by Hartmann Schopper, 1568.

Evolution of Style

This study will not touch upon works undertaken during the first Iron Age (the so-called Halstatt period, 750–450 B.C.E.) or the second Iron Age (the La Tène period, from 450 B.C.E. until the conquest of Gaul, 58–52 B.C.E.). It is during this latter period that Celtic blacksmiths proved themselves to be masters of ironwork.

Excavations undertaken in France uncovered highly perfected works and tools. As early as the first century B.C.E., the ironsmith had given a fixed form to tools; anvils, stakes, various hammers, pliers, files, and so on were the same then as their modern-day equivalents. Numerous utilitarian objects such as horseshoes, swivels, chandeliers, and locks inspired themes in the ironsmith's work, while jewelry, buckles, torques, and belt buckles were more refined. The marvelous andirons from the museum in St.-Germain reveal unequaled artisanry. These objects owe their apparent modernism to the simplification imposed by the techniques. However, in the beginning of the fifth century C.E., invasions halted the realization of these works and destroyed a large number of them. It wasn't until the twelfth century, after the fear surrounding the first millennium, that ironworks with an artistic character came back on the scene in France.

The chart on the following spread organizes the evolution of technique and style between the twelfth and nineteenth centuries.

This period can be divided into two major phases:

- the first, from the twelfth to the sixteenth centuries;
- the second, from the seventeenth to the nineteenth centuries.

Both periods have certain common characteristics: They begin with a search for the purely linear, where only suppleness and purity of line direct the design, and gradually develop into overcharged ornamentation in which filled space outweighs empty space.

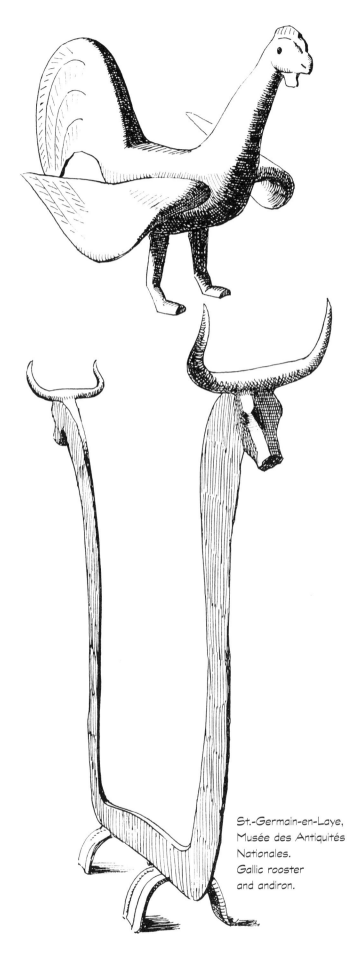

St.-Germain-en-Laye, Musée des Antiquités Nationales. Gallic rooster and andiron.

PERIOD	MATERIAL	TECHNIQUE	SCROLLWORK
12th century	Iron bars hammered to size.	Forge welding. Collars. Swelled joints. Layering. Forged ornamentation molded with a hammer.	Tight scrolls. Sometimes ending in an *eye*.
13th century	Iron bars hammered and molded in a swage.	Stamping. Mortise and tenon. Iron on the flat.	Open scrolls tipped with a stamped element.
14th–15th centuries	Same as above. Ornamental cut sheet elements. Lightly accentuated contours.	Half-lap joints. Mortise and tenon. Screws. Rivets. Filing. Piercing. Orbe-voie work.	Few scrolls. Mostly quatrefoils.
16th century	Hammered iron. Sheet metal. Water-powered hammer.	Same (except orbe-voie). Mostly repoussé and engraved sheet metal.	Very open scrolls.
Louis XIII 17th century	Mostly flat irons. Sheet metal. Rolling mill for billets in 1615.	Molded collars called *knots*. Riveted collars. Appliqué sheet metal, riveted to the irons. Swaged seeds and pistils.	Tapered scrolls terminating in *snub end*, or tight eyes.
Louis XIV	Same as above. Thicker irons. Moldings with layered irons. Gilding.	Same as above Dowelled sheet metal riveted to irons. Half-lap joints.	Sometimes elements branch from the main scroll and not the core. Protruding core, *bolt end*.
Louis XV 18th century	Hot rolled bars (stock in various profiles), 1750. Iron casting, 1722, by Réaumur.	Few collars, some balls. Rounding to reinforce corners. Brazing (rarely used). Cast elements appear.	Ram's horn.
Louis XVI	Often polished iron. Cast elements.	Much less repoussé sheet metal.	Sometimes double or triple scrolls circling out from the core. "Greek"
Empire	Mostly cast.	Only cast elements.	Few scrolls. Enlarged core.

PALMWORK	LEAFWORK	DECORATION OVERVIEW
	Carved, flat designs, few examples.	Repetitive patterns between uprights. Effect obtained from the contrast of differently sized scrolls and by heavier cross sections.
	Stamped leafwork.	Repetitive patterns. A heavier look (flat iron). Effect obtained from stamped elements.
	Ornamental cut sheet metal. Lightly accentuated contours.	Repetitive patterns. Series of bars. Friezes in cut sheet metal. Effect obtained through a contrast of curves and straight lines.
Repoussé.	Engraved ribbing.	Patterns are repetitive or arranged in horizontal bands. Few grilles, mostly locks and bolts executed in repoussé sheet metal.
	Sharply cut ornaments. Light contours. Intermittent ribbing.	Patterns in horizontal bands or panels. Few elements in sheet metal, contours are spare. Effects obtained with lines.
Corner→	Carving: ogee or ogival arches. Often a curl.	Symmetrical patterns. Contrasting lines and curves. Elements in repoussé sheet metal, contours become broader. Effects obtained from dividing the decorated surfaces.
No straight lines.	Rococo motifs. Lively. Deeply cut circular elements.	Symmetrical or asymmetrical patterns. Triumph of curved lines. Rococo motifs. Elements in repoussé sheet metal and sometimes cast ornaments. Effect obtained from the suppleness of the curves.
	Rounded carvings or lowered arch. Ribbing done in relief.	Geometric patterns. Inspiration from antiquity. Cold character, often heavy, made heavier by the use of cast elements. Effect created by dividing the groupings.
Cast.	Cast. Little relief. Spare contours.	Inspiration from antiquity. Styles are often mixed. Colder and heavier character than under Louis XVI.

25

Leafwork

The analysis of foliage cut and contour allows for easier classification of ironwork. Leafwork becomes common starting in the seventeenth century, but ironsmiths were using leafwork well before this period. In the twelfth century, grille cresting was enhanced with flat, broadly cut palms. The Abbey of St. Foy in Conques offers the earliest example of an opposing design, made of sheet metal with the fineness of iron. In the thirteenth century, stamped elements, leaves, and flowers embellished grilles and strap hinges. Numerous works executed in the nineteenth century under Viollet-le-Duc can, however, lead to confusion. These works are identifiable by their cold character and uniformity of design.

Timid attempts at cut sheet metal with rough contours crown the grilles of Langeac and St.-Sernin in Toulouse (end of the fourteenth and beginning of the fifteenth centuries). The technique of piercing introduced, at the same time, floral composition into the design of locks, knockers, and small strap hinges. Originally, these were pieces of cut sheet metal whose superimposition created a relief. Cut-out clovers were often juxtaposed on the designs. At the end of the fifteenth and beginning of the sixteenth centuries, thistles start to figure in ornamentation; the veining was engraved, and a delicate contour was pressed into the form.

In the sixteenth century, repoussé was used to decorate locks, bolts, and knockers; grilles were rare and leafing was seldom worked into ornamentation. Where iron pieces intersect and on collars, an element in sheet metal (a flower or leaf) offers a rich decorative opportunity. On the Grille aux Pampres, at the château of Blois, vines inspired the ironsmith; they entwine themselves around the rungs. Leaves and grapes were treated with a natural effect. One can still find elaborately carved leaves, achieved by a flattening of the iron, with an interior engraved design spreading out along the ends of the round-iron scrolls. It is curious to note that, in the few grilles from the sixteenth century, the master-repousseurs of the Renaissance used only flat leafwork with no contours.

In the seventeenth century, a slight evolution occurred. Leafwork performed in Louis XIII style was discreet. The delicate cut was characterized by embracing arches that had at the center a small decorative ball that caught the light. The ribbing was rough, either in relief or hollowed out, and there were no cut-outs, or peek holes, in the leaves that communicated with the exterior. The appliqué leafwork of this time was placed on iron rods with rivets that had pronounced heads. At the beginning of Louis XIV's reign, ironsmiths were treating leafwork as a common design strategy: silhouettes became less meager; embracing arches, less pronounced, were often replaced with an intersecting cut; the contour was ribbed and more refined; the veins in the leaves stretched out and faded gently; and often a gentle curve was added to the tip of the leaf. Peek holes were added and were sometimes bordered with rounded "lips" or enhanced with relief patterns that matched the rhythm of the veining. The leafwork sometimes wrapped around the iron, but it was almost always applied with visible rivets.

In the eighteenth century, the silhouette changed. Under Louis XV, the numerous and supple cuts became rounded. A ridge often jutted from the top of the leaf. The veining detail was more extensive and finely contoured and peek holes were even wider. Leafwork was frequently created in several separate pieces, assembled with hidden rivets. The arrangement was still done in appliqué, but with matted seams. Rocaille was one of the principal characteristics of this style. Elements in repoussé sheet metal were widely used. The style under Louis XVI was reminiscent of earlier styles. The cut was inspired by the technique practiced under Louis XIV, but in a colder, more reasoned, and almost mathematical manner. The contours were soft; a pronounced "knob" relief was sometimes elongated by engraved veining, called *coup de pouce.* This method has been taken up by contemporary repoussé artisans in order to create Louis XVI leafwork.

At the beginning of the nineteenth century, under the Empire style, the trend that had started under Louis XVI further evolved, and pressed sheet metal designs gave way to cast-iron motifs.

Contemporary ironsmiths are also beginning to abandon this beautiful technique because of the fragility of sheet metal ornamentation and its high cost.

14th, 15th, 16th centuries

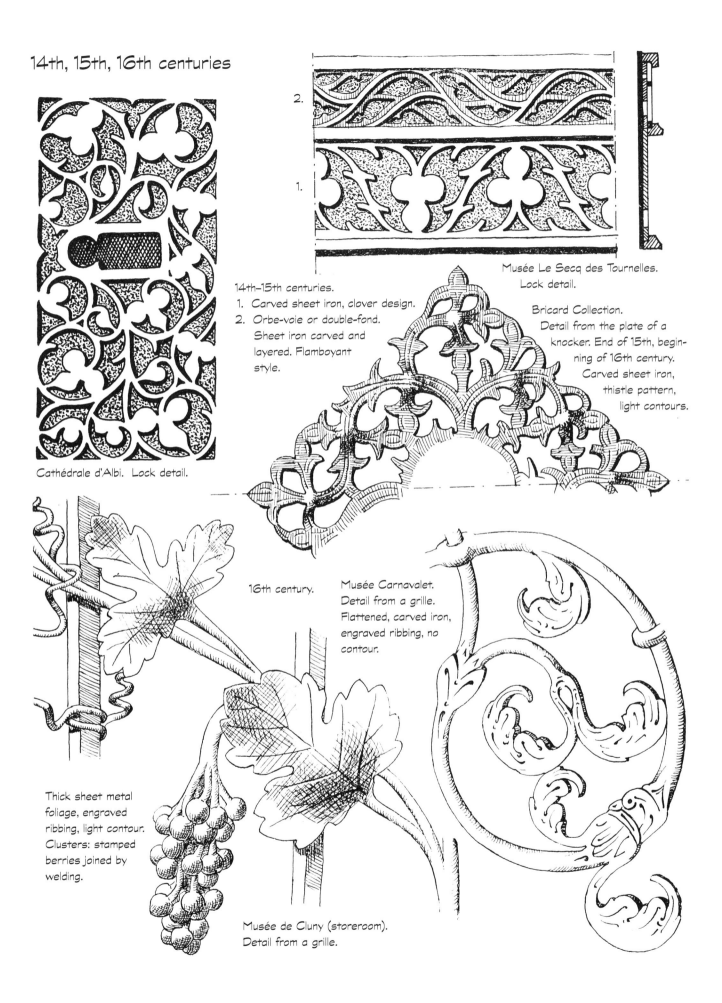

Cathédrale d'Albi. Lock detail.

14th–15th centuries.
1. Carved sheet iron, clover design.
2. Orbe-voie or double-fond. Sheet iron carved and layered. Flamboyant style.

Musée Le Secq des Tournelles. Lock detail.

Bricard Collection.
Detail from the plate of a knocker. End of 15th, beginning of 16th century. Carved sheet iron, thistle pattern, light contours.

16th century.

Musée Carnavalet. Detail from a grille. Flattened, carved iron, engraved ribbing, no contour.

Thick sheet metal foliage, engraved ribbing, light contour. Clusters: stamped berries joined by welding.

Musée de Cluny (storeroom). Detail from a grille.

17th century. Louis XIII—early Louis XIV.

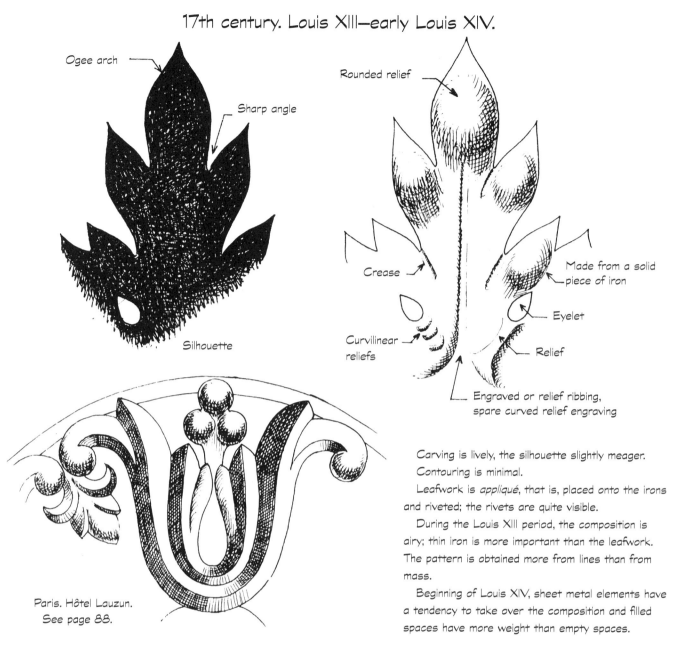

Ogee arch

Sharp angle

Silhouette

Rounded relief

Crease

Curvilinear reliefs

Made from a solid piece of iron

Eyelet

Relief

Engraved or relief ribbing, spare curved relief engraving

Paris. Hôtel Lauzun.
See page 88.

Carving is lively, the silhouette slightly meager. Contouring is minimal.

Leafwork is *appliqué*, that is, placed onto the irons and riveted; the rivets are quite visible.

During the Louis XIII period, the composition is airy; thin iron is more important than the leafwork. The pattern is obtained more from lines than from mass.

Beginning of Louis XIV, sheet metal elements have a tendency to take over the composition and filled spaces have more weight than empty spaces.

Tours. Eglise des Minimes. See page 71.

Appliqué leafwork riveted onto the irons.

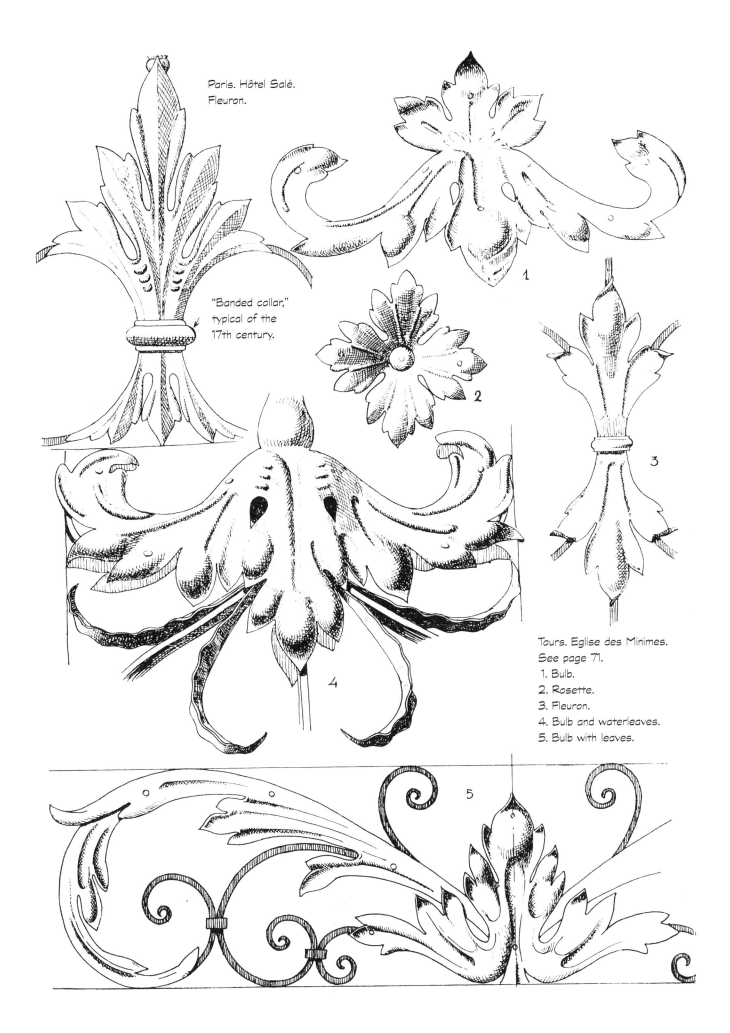

Paris. Hôtel Salé.
Fleuron.

"Banded collar,"
typical of the
17th century.

1

2

3

4

Tours. Eglise des Minimes.
See page 71.
1. Bulb.
2. Rosette.
3. Fleuron.
4. Bulb and waterleaves.
5. Bulb with leaves.

5

17th century. Louis XIV.

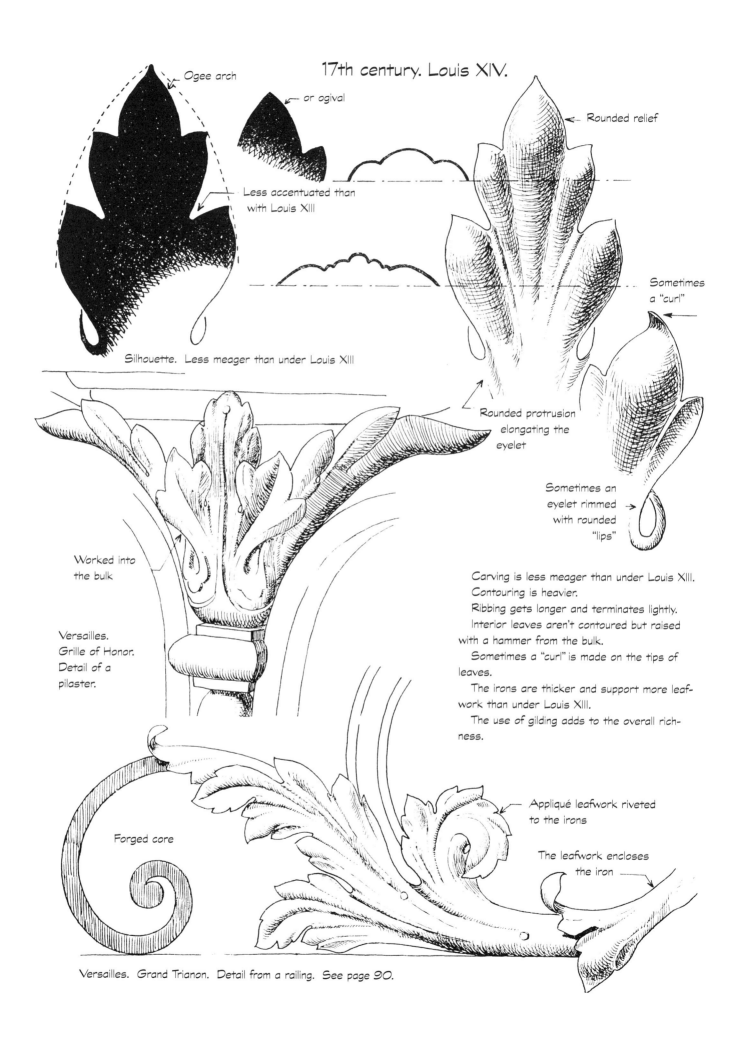

Ogee arch

or ogival

Rounded relief

Less accentuated than with Louis XIII

Silhouette. Less meager than under Louis XIII

Sometimes a "curl"

Rounded protrusion elongating the eyelet

Sometimes an eyelet rimmed with rounded "lips"

Worked into the bulk

Versailles. Grille of Honor. Detail of a pilaster.

Carving is less meager than under Louis XIII. Contouring is heavier.

Ribbing gets longer and terminates lightly.

Interior leaves aren't contoured but raised with a hammer from the bulk.

Sometimes a "curl" is made on the tips of leaves.

The irons are thicker and support more leaf-work than under Louis XIII.

The use of gilding adds to the overall richness.

Forged core

Appliqué leafwork riveted to the irons

The leafwork encloses the iron

Versailles. Grand Trianon. Detail from a railing. See page 90.

30

Worked into
the bulk

Chateau de Versailles.
Detail from a
balcony.

Shell

A

B

C

D

Worked into the bulk

Garland of flowers on a stem
stamped with seeds.

Grand Trianon.
Detail from a railing.

31

Louis XV

Crest

Sometimes a
wide curl

Raised edge

Several cuttings with
a rounded silhouette.

Rarely is there symmetry.

All lines are supple and sinuous; there are
no straight lines.

The relief, quite lively, contrasts with the
rounded silhouette of the contours.

Ribbing, quite prolific, is either in relief or
chased and thins out as it lengthens.

Eyelets are generally lined with thick "lips."

The tops of leaves often have a crest.

Mortise

Sens Cathédrale

Nancy. Rosette.

Amiens Cathédrale

Waterleaf

Asymmetrical bulb

Rouen. St.-Ouen.
Symmetrical bulbs.

33

Nancy. Place Stanislas.
Rococo elements.

Louis XV

Nancy. Place Stanislas.

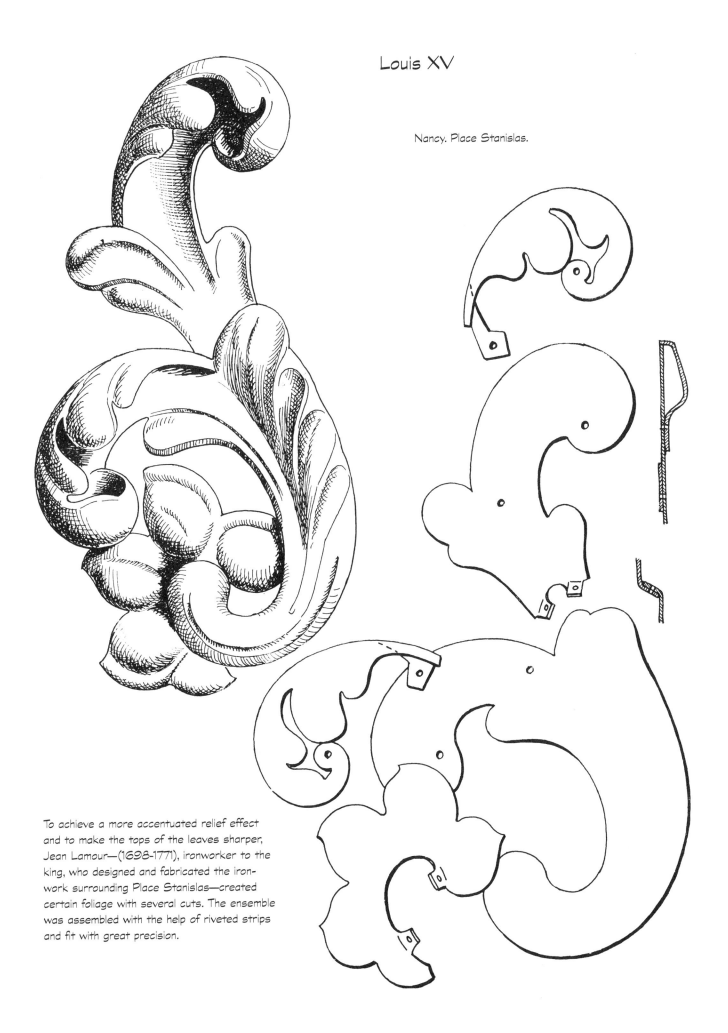

To achieve a more accentuated relief effect and to make the tops of the leaves sharper, Jean Lamour—(1698-1771), ironworker to the king, who designed and fabricated the ironwork surrounding Place Stanislas—created certain foliage with several cuts. The ensemble was assembled with the help of riveted strips and fit with great precision.

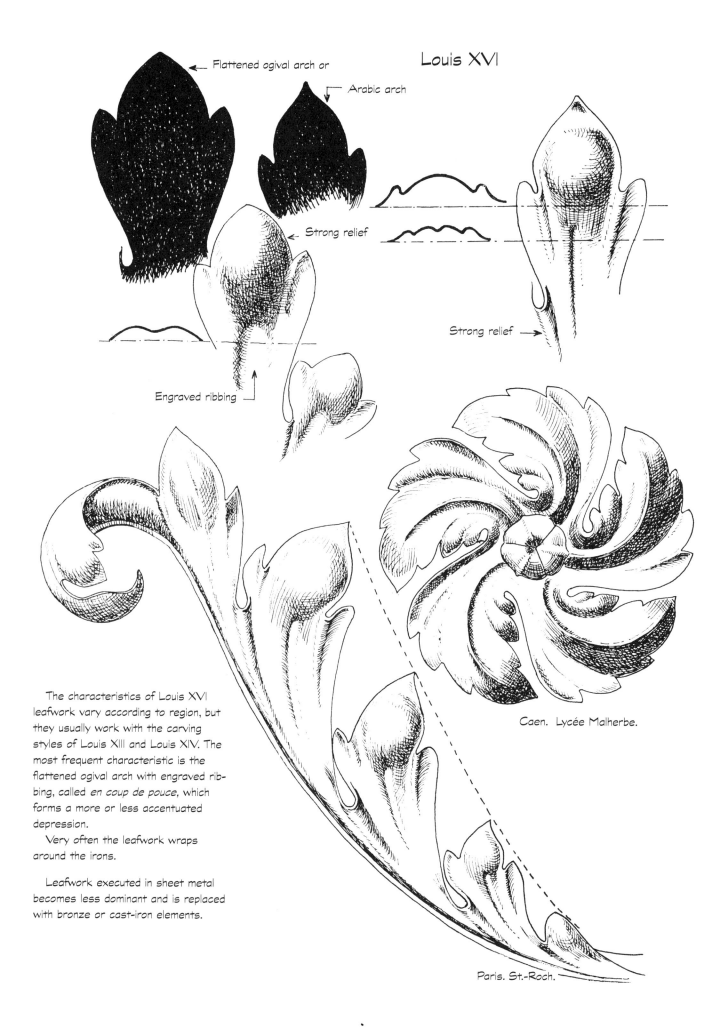

Louis XVI

Flattened ogival arch or

Arabic arch

Strong relief

Strong relief

Engraved ribbing

Caen. Lycée Malherbe.

The characteristics of Louis XVI leafwork vary according to region, but they usually work with the carving styles of Louis XIII and Louis XIV. The most frequent characteristic is the flattened ogival arch with engraved ribbing, called *en coup de pouce*, which forms a more or less accentuated depression.

Very often the leafwork wraps around the irons.

Leafwork executed in sheet metal becomes less dominant and is replaced with bronze or cast-iron elements.

Paris. St.-Roch.

36

The cut of this leafwork
resembles Louis XIV style.

Strap Hinges and Iron Fittings

Strap hinges allow a door to rotate, hold the assembly together, and maintain a right-angled construction. They are made up of a branch or band fixed onto a door, perpendicular to the axis of the opening; they terminate in a rolled eye that rotates on the tip of a sealed hinge attached to the wall. Doors were suspended with these bands, which were called strap hinges (French, *penture,* from the Latin "pendere," to hang). In certain cases, strap hinges without the eye at the end served no other purpose than to hold the joined planks together on the framework, such as on a door or chest. They were therefore called false strap hinges or *iron fittings.* Pin nails bordering interior crosspieces guaranteed the overall strength of the assembly. These nails had either one or two points and the head of the nail was the object of extensive decorative refinement. In order not to scratch the wood, a washer held the nail away from the carpentry work. Red-tinted leather inserted between the wood and the iron also protected doors.

History

The prevalence of strap hinges on the doors of cathedrals, basilicas, churches, abbeys, and the like in the Middle Ages attests to their importance at that time; ironsmiths discovered an entire mode of ornamentation through this technical necessity.

In contrast, at the beginning of the Renaissance, advances in carpentry and the abundance of sculptures and moldings relegated strap hinges to a secondary position.

The oldest preserved strap hinges from France date back to the eleventh century.

Five major varieties in France can be discerned:

1. In Auvergne, strap hinges were formed in horizontal bands highlighting vertical elements, divided in the midsection by a diamond-shaped ornament with tips decorated with human and animal heads and terminating in wide C-shaped scrolls.

   Le Puy, Brioude, Auzon, Le Dorat (where you can still find bits of protective leather under the iron or between the iron and the wooden door), Billom, Compains, Ebreuil, Lanobre, Orcival, Neuvy-Saint-Sépulcre, and Gannat.

2. In the Pyrénées-Orientales region, the design is tighter. Horizontal bands of flat iron with raised edges are split on their ends to form a double scroll; a series of tightly rolled symmetrical scrolls shoot out from these bands.

   Palalda, Coustouges, Marcevol, St.-Féliu-d'Amont, La Trinité, Corneilla-de-Conflent, Eus, Odeillo, Prades, Prats-de-Mollo (restored), Belpuig, Serralongue, Vinca.

3. In the Ile-de-France region, in Burgundy and Provence, stamping was the favored technique. The strap was formed by a series of bars held together from section to section with collars that hid the welded seams. These bars branched out in scrolls decorated with various animals and plants, executed by stamping.

   Paris: the St.-Anne doorway on Notre-Dame. In the Yonne region: Vézelay, Pontigny, Sens. In Provence: St.-Gilles-du-Gard, St.-Trophine, in Arles.

4. In Alsace, strap hinges were executed in pounded, cut, and chiseled iron. The branches divided into three parts from which sprang flowers and leaves.

5. In Anjou, false strap hinges, in flat iron, form a repetitive design with cruciform elements contrasting with diamond- and C-shapes. The decorated tips had heads that were contoured with a hammer.

   In the Maine-et-Loire region: St.-Maurice, in Angers, Fontevrault. In the Charente-Maritime region: Esnandes.

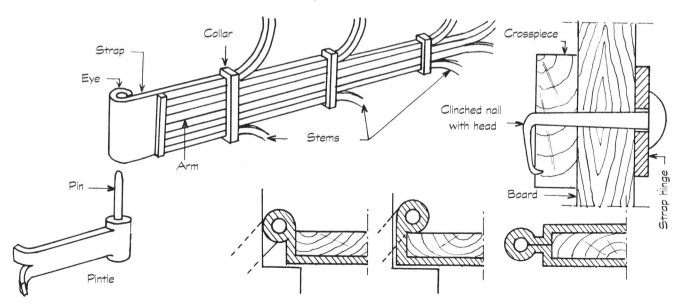

Small Strap Hinges

During the Middle Ages, strap hinges less prominent than those on church doors were used on the frames of apartment doors, as well as to hold in place and facilitate the rotation of shutters, cupboard doors, and sideboard doors.

Strap hinges on doors, executed in thick sheet metal, were generally composed of two rectangular plates tied together with a central hinge. The mounting on the doorframe required these rectangles to be placed high up. Only their ends were decorated. Frame assembly was infrequently held together at an angle.

Interior shutters, with one or two leaves, protected the casement. The two leaves on a shutter could be folded separately or moved together within a moving frame attached to the doorframe. Each problem had a different solution.

The part of the strap hinge fixed to the doorframe was often T-shaped or at a right angle. The branch, set on a hinge, was long and could fold back on itself to form a "couple" on shutters with two leaves.

Design elements were generally located on the ends, but the branch was sometimes pierced with a simple pattern. Armoire and buffet strap hinges, called credenza strap hinges, were simpler. They were almost always made up of a long, articulated arm on a wider piece that folded back on the thickness of the doorframe. The cut design stood out against a red background. In the fourteenth century, a single plate was pierced with a floral design.

In the fifteenth and sixteenth centuries, the design was called "double-fond" or "orbe-voie;" two (or, less frequently, three) cut plates were layered. They were held together with a border fitted with an iron rod with diagonal notches. This imitation is called a "twist."

Toward the end of the fifteenth century, the upper plate was often lightly pressed. A single cut plate decorated with pressed thistles, gently engraved, represents the type of strap hinge common in the sixteenth century.

Examples of strap hinges later than the sixteenth century are unusual. From this period on, this logical means of suspension was generally hidden rather than highlighted.

There are interesting examples of armoire strap hinges: from the twelfth century, in Aubazine (Corrèze); from the thirteenth century, at the Bayeux cathedral; from the fourteenth century, at the Abbey of Selongey (Côte d'Or) and in the Musée des Arts Décoratifs, in Paris, the Mont-Saint-Quentin armoire; from the fifteenth century, in Le Chalard (Haute-Vienne).

You can also see shutter hinges at the Musée de Cluny Paris, in the Bricard Collection, and, in the Fontevrault-L'Abbaye (Maine-et-Loire), a beautiful model for strap hinges for a door with a curved top dating from the sixteenth century.

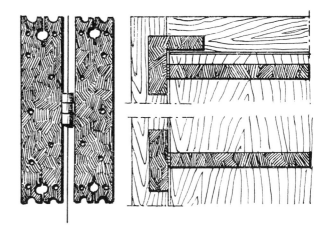

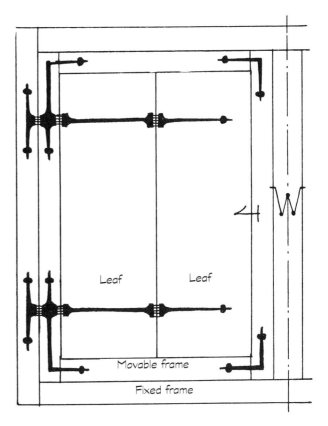

Leaf   Leaf

Movable frame

Fixed frame

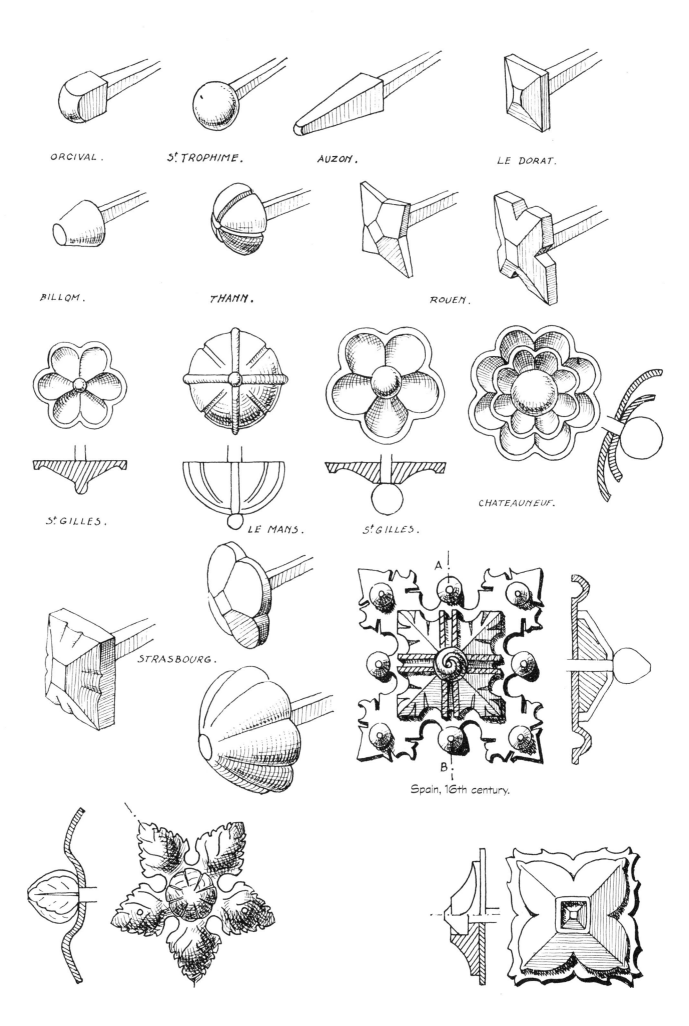

ORCIVAL.

St. TROPHIME.

AUZON.

LE DORAT.

BILLOM.

THANN.

ROUEN.

St. GILLES.

LE MANS.

St. GILLES.

CHATEAUNEUF.

STRASBOURG.

A

B

Spain, 16th century.

40

Auvergne. 12th–13th centuries.

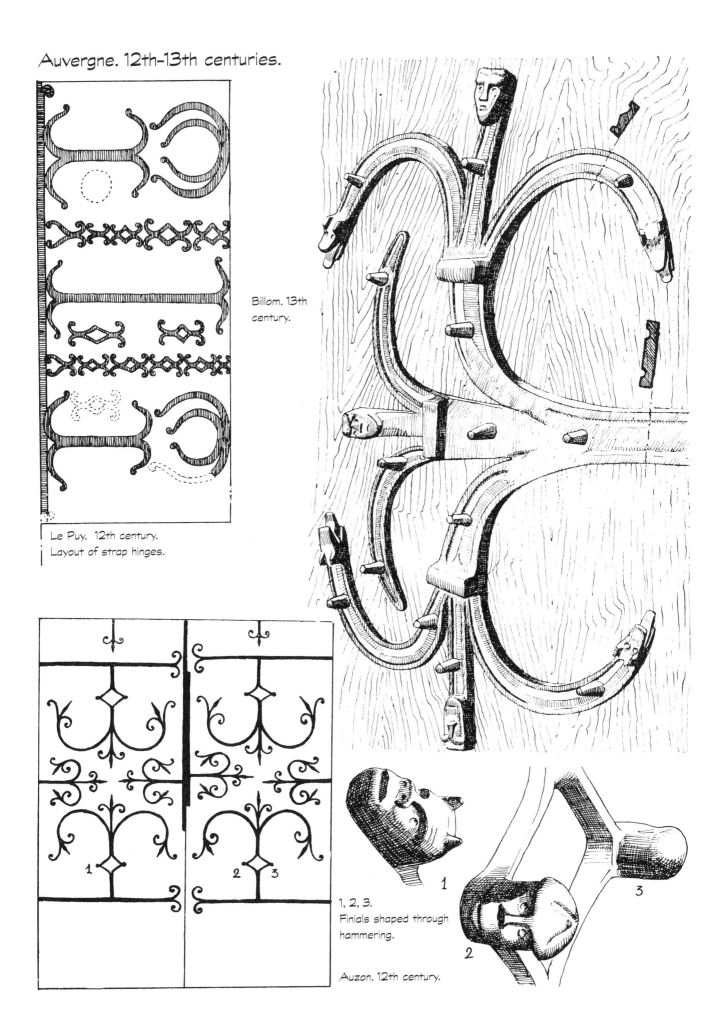

Le Puy. 12th century.
Layout of strap hinges.

Billom. 13th century.

1, 2, 3.
Finials shaped through hammering.

Auzon. 12th century.

Pyrénées-Orientales. 12th century.

Marcevol. Layout and
detail of strap hinges.

A. Half-lap assembly.

Serralongue. Details.

B. Welded.
C. Welded collar.
D. "Rolled eye" with space for nails.

B - C

42

Provence. 13th century.

St.-Gilles du Gard.

Arles. Saint-Trophime.

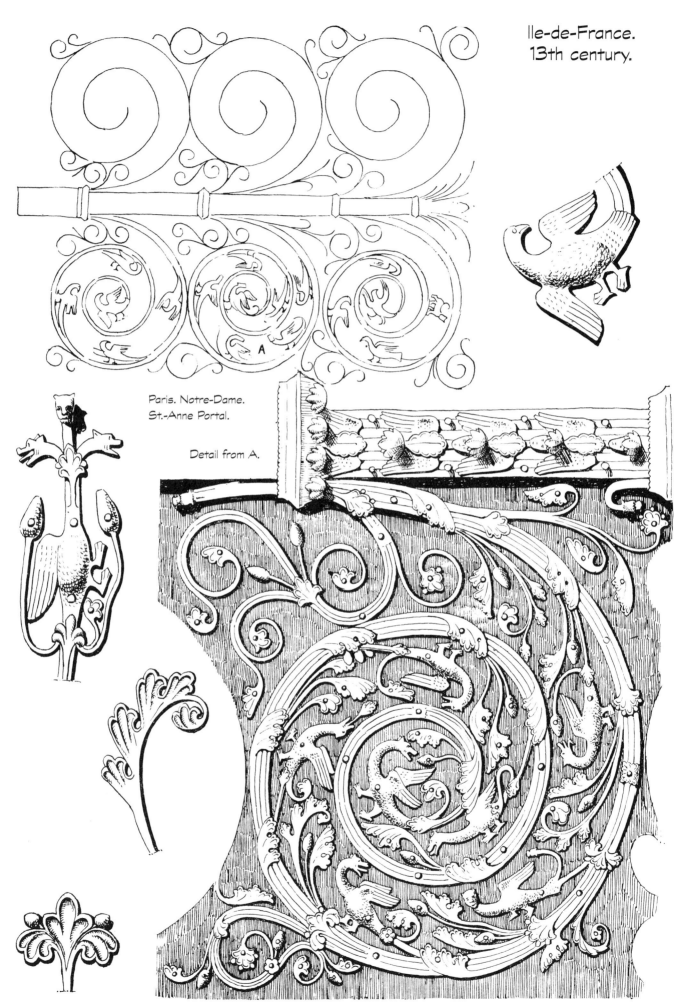

Ile-de-France.
13th century.

Paris. Notre-Dame.
St.-Anne Portal.

Detail from A.

44

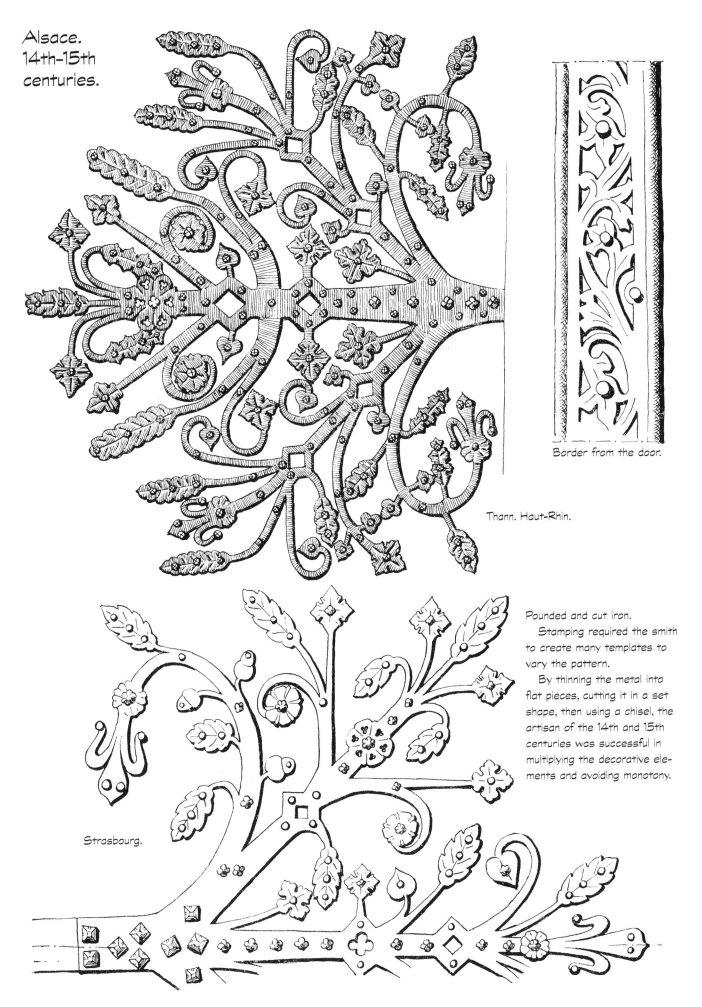

Alsace.
14th-15th
centuries.

Border from the door.

Thann. Haut-Rhin.

Strasbourg.

Pounded and cut iron.

Stamping required the smith
to create many templates to
vary the pattern.

By thinning the metal into
flat pieces, cutting it in a set
shape, then using a chisel, the
artisan of the 14th and 15th
centuries was successful in
multiplying the decorative elements and avoiding monotony.

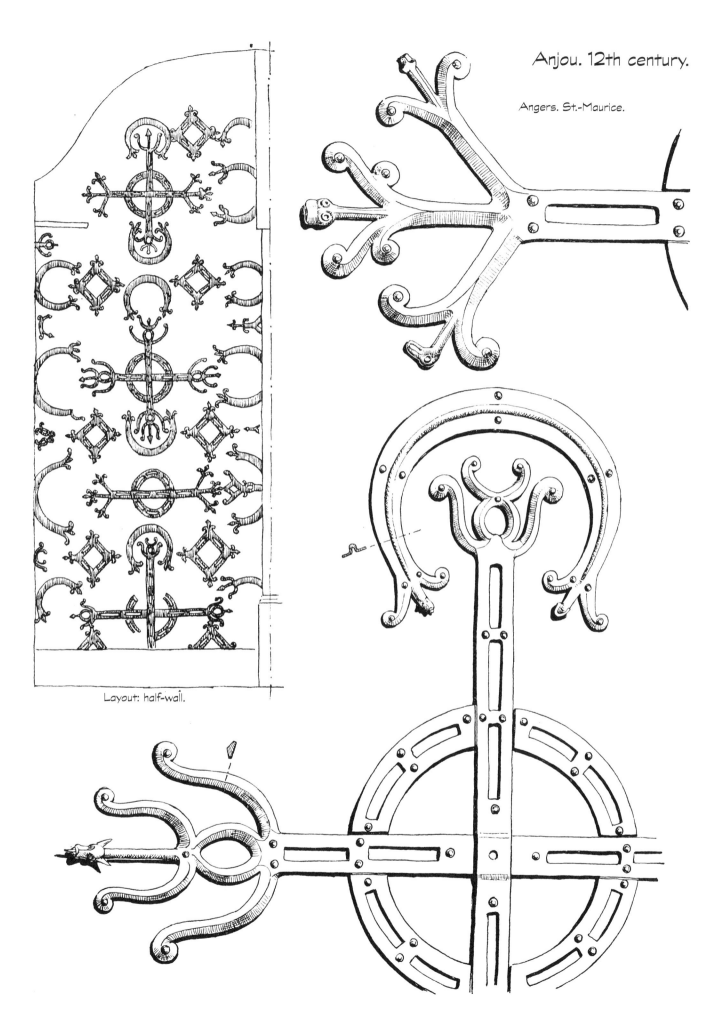

Anjou. 12th century.

Angers. St.-Maurice.

Layout: half-wall.

46

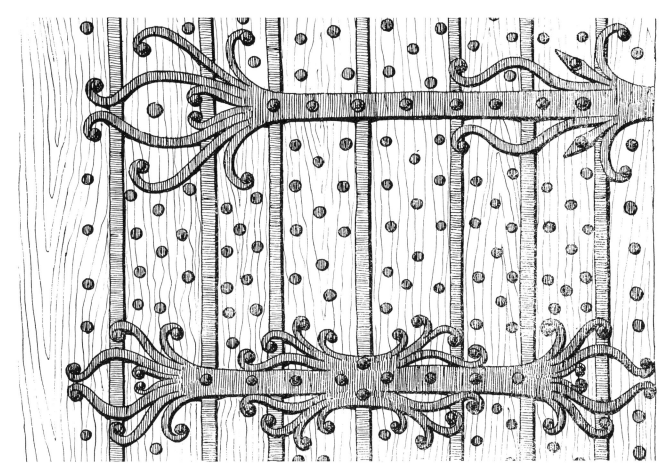

Bayeux. Cathedral. 14th–15th centuries.

End of 14th–beginning of 15th century.
Pierced metal flower pattern.

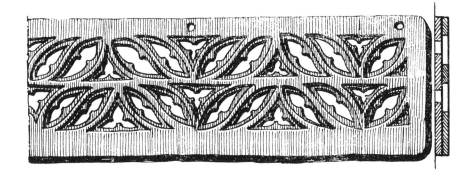

End of 14th–15th centuries.
Orbe-voie or double-fond. Two
or three layered plates. Flamboyant
pattern.

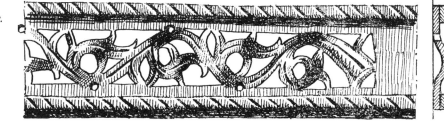

End of 15th–beginning of 16th century.
Pierced metal, engraved and
repoussé. Thistle pattern. The plate
has an iron border—known as a
twist—made with notches.

47

Iron Fixtures for Chests

Chests were made up of posts acting as feet and cross sections that formed the sides, the back, and the lid. The ensemble was, in the Middle Ages, connected with iron straps or bands in the form of scrolling branches, usually decorated with stamped designs. In the figure below are:

A. Corner straps, which hold the crosspieces to the posts and preserve the overall right angles.

B. Bands holding the cross sections together and holding the bottom.

C. Hinges holding the cover and allowing it to open. These hinges were eventually placed on the interior to prevent burglary.

D. Straps with a latched end. This was made up of a keeper, or staple, through which the bolt of the lock passed to ensure the locking of the cover.

The chest, or coffer, in the Middle Ages was the only piece of furniture that offered adequate security for the storage of valuable objects. It could also serve as a chair or even a bed or table, and it helped with moving, hence the care given to its construction.

In the twelfth and thirteenth centuries, because coffer assembly was not solid enough, coffers were reinforced with iron hinges. These made the case stronger, allowed for the cover to swing open, and added to the overall ornamentation.

Eventually, progress in woodworking relegated iron hinges to a secondary role; as early as the fifteenth century, designs were sculpted or achieved with embossed leather or with a painted cloth lining.

Individuals interested in old chests should visit the Musée Carnavalet, the Musée de Cluny, and the Musée des Arts Décoratifs, in Paris.

There are still chests characteristic of the thirteenth century in Chitry (Yonne); from the fourteenth and fifteenth centuries, in the Noyon cathedral (Oise); from the sixteenth century, in Rozay-en-Brie (Seine-et-Marne) and in Villemaur (Aube).

Welding joints camouflaged by checkering executed with a chisel.

Paris. Musée Carnavalet. 13th century.

Paris. Musée des Arts Décoratifs. 13th century.

1ᵐ20

0ᵐ88

Noyon. Cathedral. 15th century.

49

Grillework

A grille, or grate, is an open work designed to close off, protect, or divide without blocking light or view. Grilles, used either inside or outside, may have fixed parts, or frames, and movable parts, or openings.

Exterior Grilles

FUNCTION

A. Grille frames serve to enclose and define property, public space, and the like, or to secure an opening, a cellar window, an oeil-de-boeuf window, and so on.
B. Grilles that open are meant to allow or prevent passage, either by cars (a carriage grille, made like two doors), or by pedestrians (a single grille door or window, which may be incorporated into the carriage grille or separate from it).

Grilles that open may have a pediment above them, as at Versailles and the Palais de Justice, in Paris, or a transom, as is the case in apartment buildings.

SECURITY

A. Height. For public grilles in France, the prescribed height starts at 3.2 meters (10.5 feet) for cities with more than 50,000 inhabitants and at 2.6 meters (8.5 feet) for other towns.
B. Barring entry. The upper part of the grille should be equipped with points, spears, thorns, and so on to prevent climbing.
C. Protection. The maximum space between bars, according to French specifications, is 14 centimeters (5.5 inches).
D. Antitheft. When grilles are intended to prevent burglary, as is the case in banks, they should not have any removable parts.

Fixed or Frame Grilles

CHARACTERISTICS (fig. 1).

A. Masonry casement
B. Metal casement
C. Posts
D. Buttresses
E. Principal crosspieces
F. Intermediate crosspieces
G. Central crosspieces
H. Side wall
I. Bars
J. Frieze

The distance between posts or between casements is called the span; it should not exceed 2.5 meters (8.2 feet). The distance between the principal crosspieces, or range, should not be more than 2 meters (6.5 feet); beyond that, intermediary crosspieces are necessary (G).

CONSTRUCTION (fig. 1).

Strength: Guaranteed by masonry (A) or metal (B) casements, and by basic posts (C), buttresses (D), and, if need be, both spans.
Rigidity: Obtained with crosspieces (E, F, G). Consider the amount of iron and proportional relationships between the various elements in order to avoid swaying and bending.
Cost: Depending on the budget, half-lap joints, and welding, an economical solution—or a more arduous solution—swelled or pass-through joints, may be chosen.
Protection: Lead paint, paint, or gilding.

Composition

Bars (fig. 2):
Between 16 and 25 millimeters (0.6 and 1 inch) long or in diameter in order to resist any type of warping. Their dimension (e) dictates the other dimensions. Bars are sometimes tipped with a spear on top and a band on the bottom.

Posts (fig.3):
Basic post: $L = 2e$ (e is the thickness of the bar)
Buttressing post: $L = 5/2e$ (figs. 3 and 5)

Crosspieces (fig. 3):
$L : 2e$. Intermediate crosspieces are almost always U-shaped.

Pass-through joints (fig. 4):
Generally executed on crosspieces; the pierced member is twice the thickness of the crosspiece.

Settings (fig. 6):
a) The ends of the crosspieces in casements
b) The ends of the posts in the wall
c) The ends of the buttresses in the wall (fig. 5)

Length is a function of the materials' resistance: 40 to 50 millimeters (1.5 to 2 inches) in reinforced cement, 100 to 150 millimeters (3.9 to 5.9 inches) in brick. Design elements (A) should be removable to allow the grille and settings to be positioned.

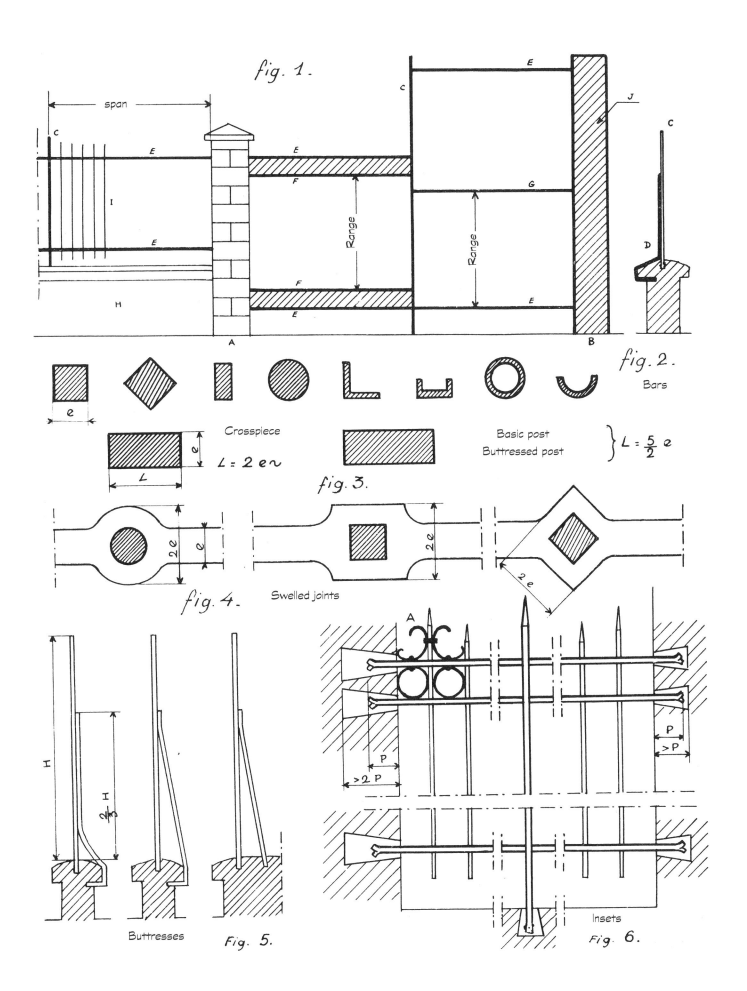

fig. 1.

span

Range

Range

fig. 2.

Bars

Crosspiece

$L = 2e$ ~

Basic post
Buttressed post $\left.\right\} L = \dfrac{5}{2} e$

fig. 3.

$2e$ e

$2e$

$2e$

fig. 4.

Swelled joints

Buttresses

Fig. 5.

Insets

Fig. 6.

51

Grilles That Open

CHARACTERISTICS:
Grilles that open allow for cars and people to pass through and offer the same security as fixed grilles. A grille pushes open from the outside. In two-paneled grilles, the one on the right opens first.

As shown in fig. 7, they may:

- have one panel or gate, minimum width 0.9 meters (3 feet)
- have two panels, width 2.5 to 3 meters (8.2 to 9.8 feet)
- have two panels with an inset gate, minimum width 4 meters (13 feet)

ESSENTIAL ELEMENTS (fig. 8):

A. Pivot post
B. Shutter-catch post
C. Crossbar
D. Crosspieces
E. Brace
F. Socket
G. Stop
H. Collars

POSTS:
The pivot post has a square cross section. The shutter-catch post, with a thickness equal to the crosspieces, is, as its name suggests, equipped with a shutter catch.

CROSSBAR (C):
The thickness is equal to that of the pivot post.

CROSSPIECES (D):
Structural members that provide a visual transition, with a single or double fillet (fig. 10).

PANEL (I):
Made of sheet metal, it is fixed between the crosspieces with an angle iron.

ROTATION:
The pivot post ends in a brace (E), which holds the axle of the socket (F) (fig. 11). On top, cylindrical pivots hold the collars (H), which hold the gate and allow it to rotate.

COLLARS (H):
They are fixed or adjustable (fig. 12). They compensate for the overall distortion of the assembly. The upper collar is placed under the upper crosspiece; the bottom collar above the intermediate crosspiece.

CLOSING:
For a double-paneled grille, two solutions are possible:
1. The left panel houses the catch and bolt, and the right holds the lock.
2. A lock bolt allows locking of both panels simultaneously.

STOPPING ELEMENTS:
- In a closed position, the panel is held by a secured stop (fig. 13), which also serves as the strike for the bolt.
- In an open position, with a swinging grille clasp or a bolt staple.

Interior Grilles

FUNCTION
In most cases, interior grilles serve merely as dividers, so it is not necessary for them to be as robust as exterior grilles. However, if they are to prevent entry, like the grilles that enclose church choirs, their characteristics are similar to those of exterior grilles.

EXECUTION
The iron may be a smaller gauge than on exterior grilles. In contrast, execution of interior grilles must be more refined, as they are more likely to be seen up close.
The inconvenience of using sheet metal and polished or hammered iron on the exterior to prevent corrosion disappears with interiors.

AESTHETICS
The same main laws of composition govern ornamentation, but general ambiance must be kept in mind in order to tie the grillework in smoothly to the overall decoration.

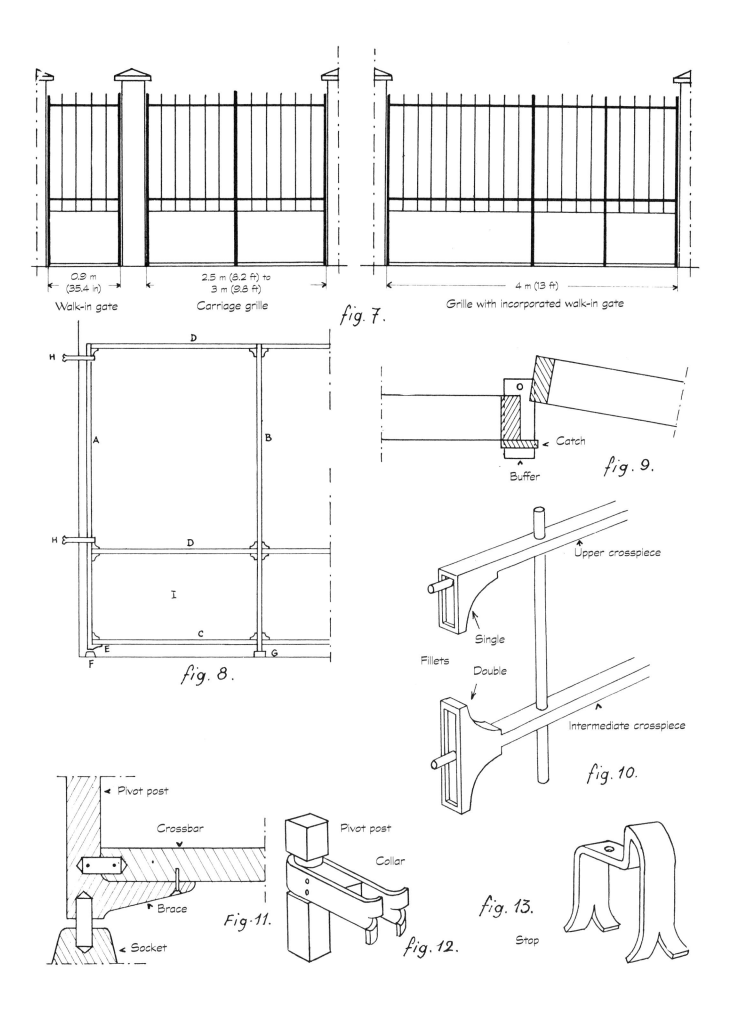

0.9 m
(35.4 in)

Walk-in gate

2.5 m (8.2 ft) to
3 m (9.8 ft)

Carriage grille

fig. 7.

4 m (13 ft)

Grille with incorporated walk-in gate

H

D

A

B

H

D

I

C

E

F

G

fig. 8.

O

Catch

Buffer

fig. 9.

Upper crosspiece

Single

Fillets

Double

Intermediate crosspiece

fig. 10.

Pivot post

Crossbar

Brace

Socket

Fig. 11.

Pivot post

Collar

fig. 12.

fig. 13.

Stop

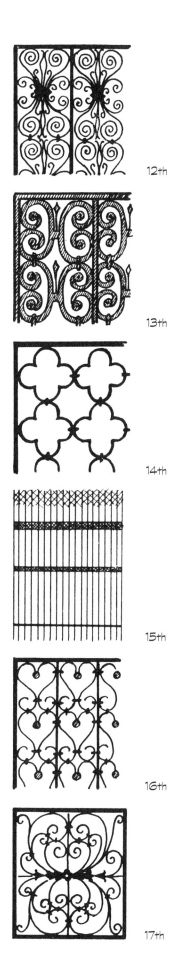

12th

13th

14th

15th

16th

17th

History of Grillework

In the eleventh and twelfth centuries, grillework design was obtained through simple repetition of small panels held between posts with collars and composed of tightly curled scrolls or C-shapes executed in flat iron. Their juxtaposition gives a central weight and develops the overall composition. As in Conques (Aveyron), a defensive crown—barbed tips—sometimes terminates the posts above the upper crosspiece. At Le Puy, punch marks have ornamented the iron.

In this area, we will mention, besides those already cited, the grillework in the churches of Billom, St.-Aventin (Haute-Garonne), at St.-Pierre de Toulouse, St.-Jean-de-Malte in Aix-en Provence, the cathedrals of Béziers (window grilles from the thirteenth century), and Noyon (a protective rose grille), which illustrate this era. The grille from the Abbey of Morigny can also be seen at the Musée d'Etampes.

In the thirteenth century, small-dimensioned grillework was composed of basic repeated patterns fixed between posts or in a frame. The design, based on open, C-shaped scrollwork, was molded. The flat side of the grille is visible and the iron is stamped on both sides. These grilles have no crowns. Some can be seen at the Musée de Cluny, in Paris, at the Musée d'Auxerre, in the crypt of the Abbey of St.-Denis, and at the cathedral of Reims.

The fourteenth and fifteenth centuries are characterized by two types of grille design. In the first, quatrefoils form patterns with basic or alternating repetitions; these quatrefoils are sometimes decorated using the stamping technique. Ornamentation in iron that has been hammered, cut, and lightly repoussé enriches the crownwork. Floral elements often serve as collars for the assembling rivets. In Paris, the Musée de Cluny houses two small grillework panels executed in this manner and the Musée des Arts Décoratifs has a double-paneled grille. In Rouen, the Musée Le Secq des Tournelles houses a grille that comes from a church in Beaujolais.

The second type of design was inspired by architecture. Executed in orbe-voie (a superimposition of varying shapes), its relief evokes carpentry and wood sculpture. The panels are hinged between the posts and crosspieces. Elements in cut-and-pressed sheet metal form crownwork of minor importance. This type of design was common in Spain. The Louvre houses a Spanish orbe-voie grille; one of the doors of the cathedral in Rouen was also executed in this style.

In the fifteenth and sixteenth centuries, grillework was made of a series of bars held by crosspieces with the help of bulge joints. Designs were made in horizontal bands, executed in cut-and-pressed sheet metal, riveted onto the crosspieces. Crownwork became more refined, as can be seen with the churches at Sarrancolin (Hautes-Pyrénées), at Belpech (Aude), and at Venerque (Haute-Garonne).

In the beginning of the seventeenth century, grilles were made of a series of bars with horizontal S-shaped and C-shaped bands, demonstrating an attempt at lightness of line and an almost complete absence of sheet metal elements.

The grilles on the church at Arreau (Hautes-Pyrénées), on the Noyon cathedral (Oise), those decorated with agricultural implements in the Musée Carnavalet, Paris, and the window grates in Besançon illustrate this decorative design.

Louis XIII-style grillework offers panels with light decoration, executed in flat iron, held in a frame. Leafwork, treated minimally, is riveted in appliqué onto the irons. Grilles from the Minimes church in Tours and the church of St.-Jean-de-Malte in Aix-en-Provence are typical examples of this style.

Louis XIV style includes two periods:

1. Until about 1660, it is still influenced by Renaissance and Louis XIII styles.
2. From 1660 onward, the classical period brings order and symmetry.

This is the beginning of major exterior works. Grillework is composed of bars topped with iron spear tips; at regular intervals, pilasters, more richly decorated, consolidate the whole.

Large opening grilles are topped with an independent pediment in the form of a "gendarme cap" placed on an entablature usually supported by flat pilasters and reinforced with buttresses. The interior work is made up of straight bars; the design, symmetrical, is laid out in horizontal and vertical bands.

These are the characteristics found on the grilles of Val-de-Grâce, in Paris, executed by Jean Mouchy and Sébastien Mathérion about 1666; at the château of Versailles, by Luchet, about 1679; at the former abbey of St.-Denis, at Cisay-Saint-Aubin (Orne); and so on.

The eighteenth century is marked by two time periods:

First, **the Louis XV era,** the style of which develops in three stages.

- The first, until about 1730, corresponds to the Regency, during which the Louis XIV style continues.
- The second, from 1730 to about 1760, sees the triumph of the rocaille style, with:

Valet: St.-Gervais, Paris (about 1741);
Nicolas Flambart: St.-Ouen, Rouen (1749);
Pierre Delphin: the hospital in Troyes (1760);
Veyrens, called Vivarais: grillework for the Amiens cathedral (1762);
and above all Jean Lamour, to whom we owe the famous grilles from the Place Stanislas and the Place Carrière, both in Nancy;
the grilles from the cathedrals of Bayeux, Bordeaux, Evreux, Sens, and Noyon.

Pediments assume a greater importance; the entablature is often curved; pilasters, four-sided, are topped with a capital inspired by antiquity. Bars are rarely continuous. The design, symmetrical or asymmetrical, resists linearity, with elements executed in sheet metal pressed with ribbed contours.

- The third stage is marked by its contrast to the outrageousness of rococo style. This is a period of transition between Louis XV and Louis XVI styles.

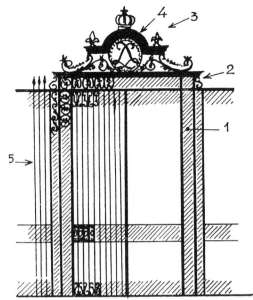

Louis XIV. Versailles. Kitchen garden.
1. Flat pilaster.
2. Horizontal entablature.
3. "Gendarme cap" pediment.
4. Molded backing.
5. Even bars.
////. Design with horizontal and vertical friezes. Symmetry.
Elements in repoussé sheet metal.

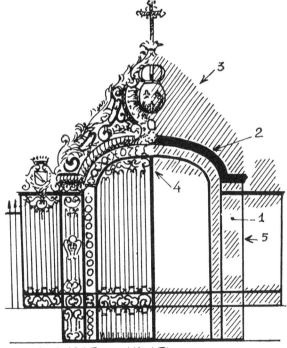

Louis XV. Troyes. Hôtel-Dieu.
1. Four-sided pilasters.
2. Rounded entablature.
3. Emphasized triangular pediment.
4. Bars rarely even.
5. Bars interrupted by patterns.
////. Symmetrical or asymmetrical design.
Elements in repoussé sheet metal.

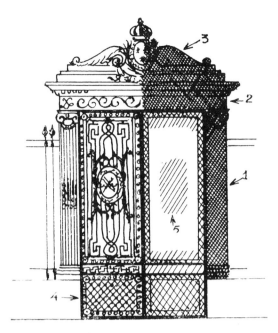

Louis XVI. Paris. Palais de Justice.
1. Squared pilaster.
2. Thick entablature, straight or curved.
3. Lower pediment.
4. Characteristic checkering.
5. Bars interrupted with patterns.
Elements in cast metal, little sheet metal.

The Louis XVI era brought about new ideas.

Grille composition became increasingly more architectural. Pilasters, entablatures, and pediments are, more often than not, heavy in appearance. The design, inspired by antiquity, gives an impression of formality and severity. Sheet metal is used less and less in favor of elements executed in cast iron and bronze. For example:

In Paris: the grillework on the Palais de Justice, executed by Bigonnet, from drawings by Desmaisons, about 1785; at the École Militaire, by Claude Fayet, based on drawings by Gabriel, about 1773; at St.-Germain-l'Auxerrois, by Pierre Dumiez, about 1767; the communion ledge at St.-Roch, by Doré, from drawings by Challe.

In Chartres: the hospital, by Pérès, about 1767.
In Bordeaux: the stock exchange, by Dumaine, about 1773.
In Nevers: the former cathedral grille, by Denis Boüe, placed at the entry to the museum about 1770.
In Dijon: the grillework on the Palais des Ducs et des États, by Meignen, called Nantua, from drawings by Le Jolivet, about 1783–85.
In Compiègne: the entry grille of the château, etc.

Empire–nineteenth century: a new style appears.

Pediments and entablatures become less important; pilasters are replaced by a series of spears that do not support the entablature. All decorative elements, inspired by antiquity, are executed in cast iron, resulting in a slender-looking ensemble.

In Nantes: the Maison des Cariatides, the Préfecture.
In Fontainebleau, at the château, the Cheval-Blanc court, about 1810.

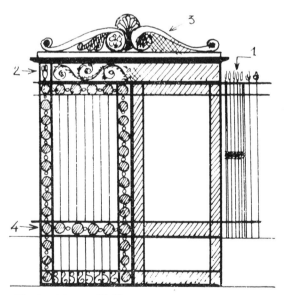

Empire. Nantes. Préfecture.
1. Bundle of spears for pilaster.
2. Horizontal entablature.
3. Lower pediment.
4. Bars interrupted with friezes.
Design in horizontal and vertical bands.
Cast elements, no sheet metal.

Description of the Crownwork on the Grilles of L'Eglise de Conques, Abbey of St. Foy, Aveyron

Nine grilles of about 3 meters (9.8 feet) in height, placed between the columns, enclose the choir. They were fabricated from the chains and shackles of prisoners who were freed thanks to the intervention of St. Foy, patron saint of the church. The saint's representation in the tympanum, prostrate beneath the hand of God, which confirms Bernard d'Angers' testimony, seems to lend weight to this traditional story. It is also possible to see, under the arcades, the chains that the freed prisoners hung in ex voto. Also on the tympanum are strap hinges and locks on the doors to Heaven and Hell.

Triple-pointed tips (A) terminate the upper part of the grille posts. Others (C), fixed onto the posts with collars, curve towards the ground and are tipped with finely contoured dragon heads. In keeping with a popular style of the period, this crownwork prevented climbing on the grille, thereby protecting the choir. The posts are assembled on crossbars with pass-through joints (D). The design as a whole, made up of small panels, is held together between the posts with collars welded shut (E). The small scrolls forming palm leaves are welded (F) onto the main designs.

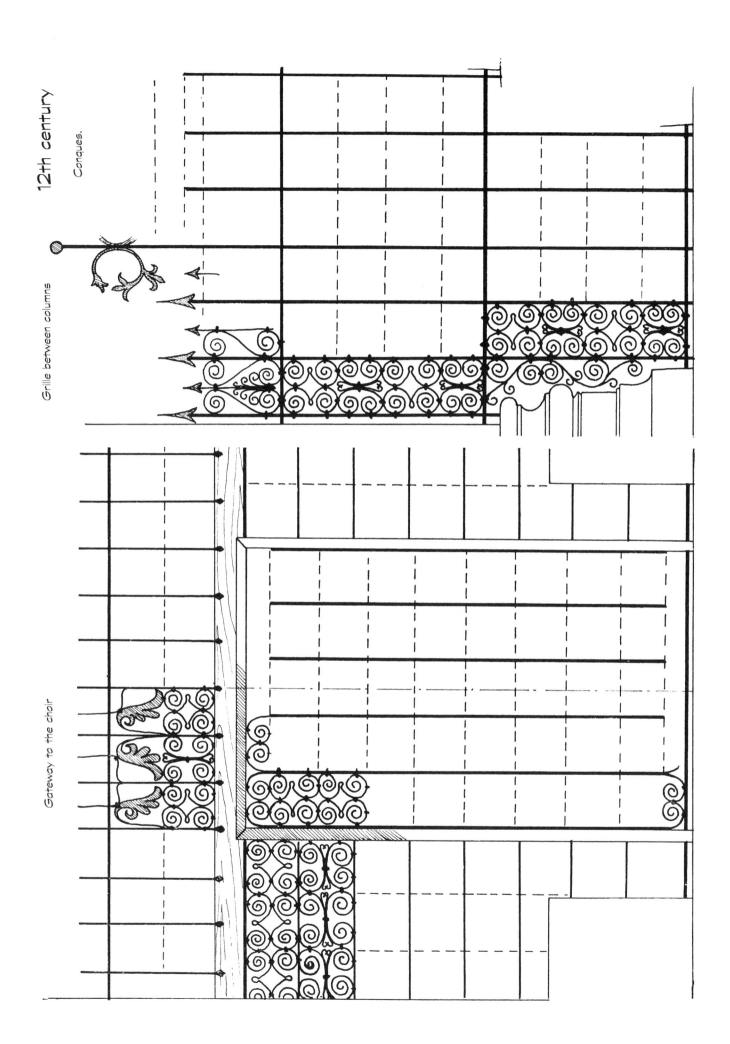

12th century

Conques.

Grille between columns

Gateway to the choir

58

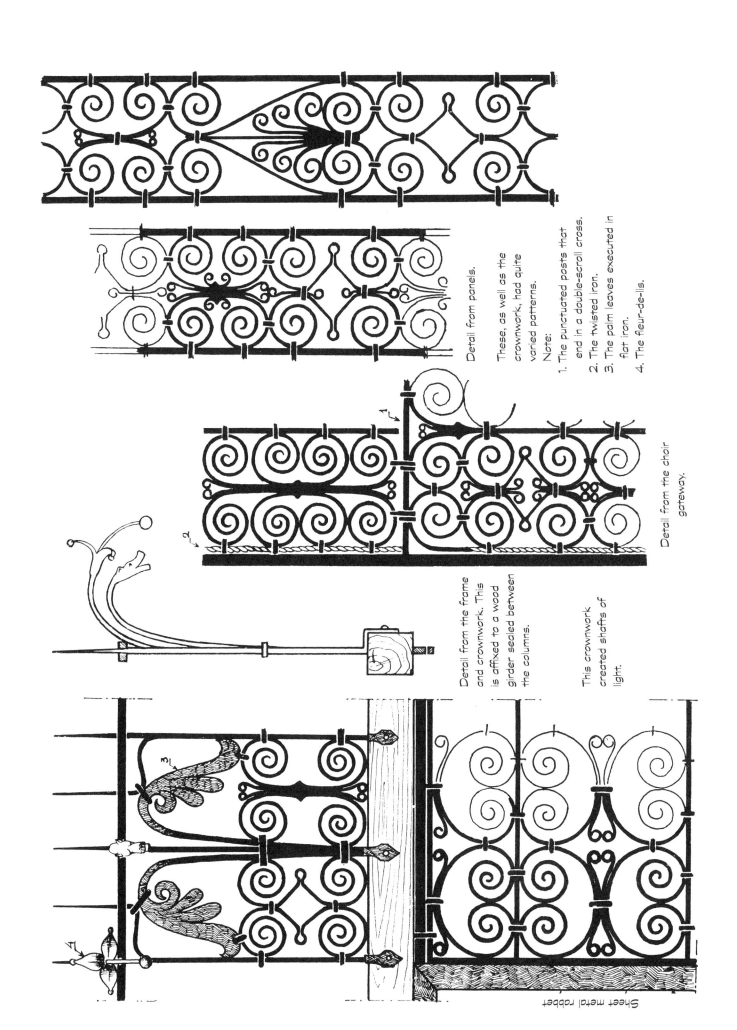

Detail from panels.

These, as well as the crownwork, had quite varied patterns.
Note:

1. The punctuated posts that end in a double-scroll cross.
2. The twisted iron.
3. The palm leaves executed in flat iron.
4. The fleur-de-lis.

Detail from the choir gateway.

Detail from the frame and crownwork. This is affixed to a wood girder sealed between the columns.

This crownwork created shafts of light.

Sheet metal rabbet

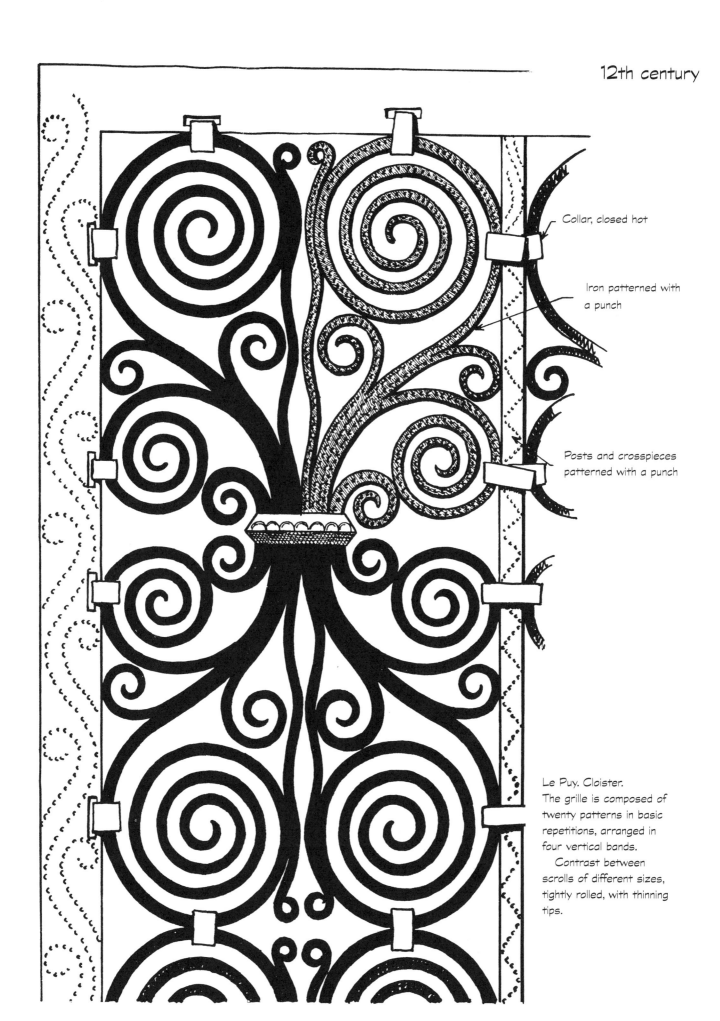

Collar, closed hot

Iron patterned with
a punch

Posts and crosspieces
patterned with a punch

Le Puy. Cloister.
The grille is composed of
twenty patterns in basic
repetitions, arranged in
four vertical bands.
    Contrast between
scrolls of different sizes,
tightly rolled, with thinning
tips.

Beginning of the
13th century

Rouen. Musée Le Secq des Tournelles.
Grille from the abbey of Ourscamp.

Scrolls tipped with a rolled eyelet.

Scrolls of different sizes and irons of variable thickness are layered to create a lacework effect.

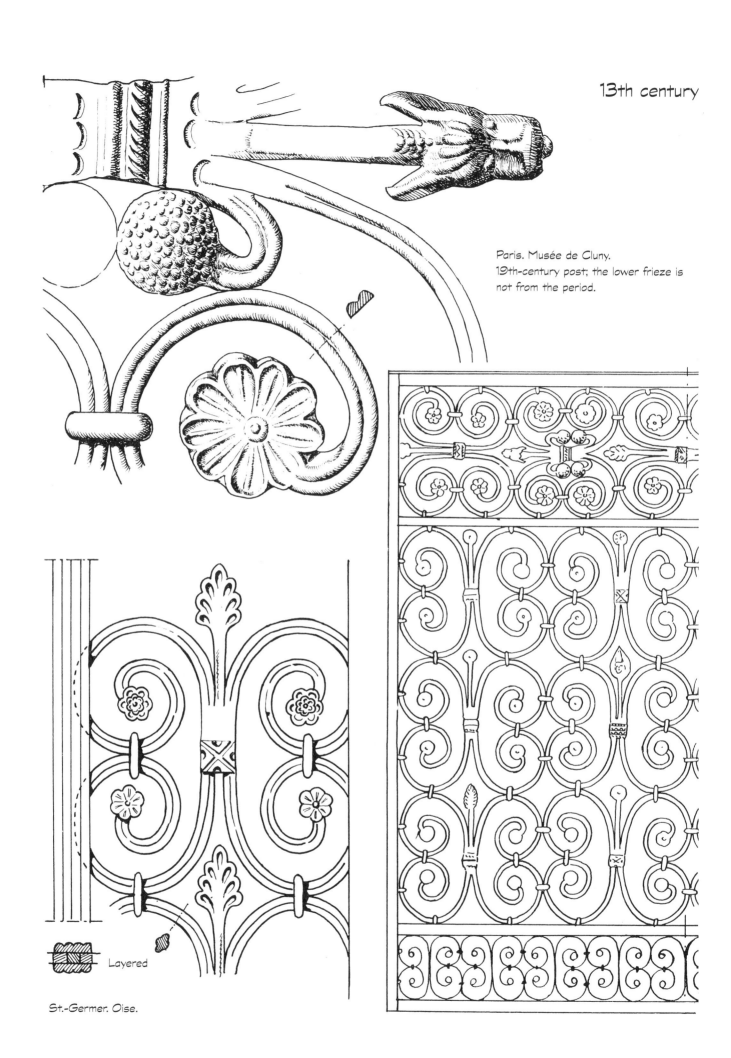

visible at top right

13th century

Paris. Musée de Cluny.
19th-century post; the lower frieze is
not from the period.

Layered

St.-Germer. Oise.

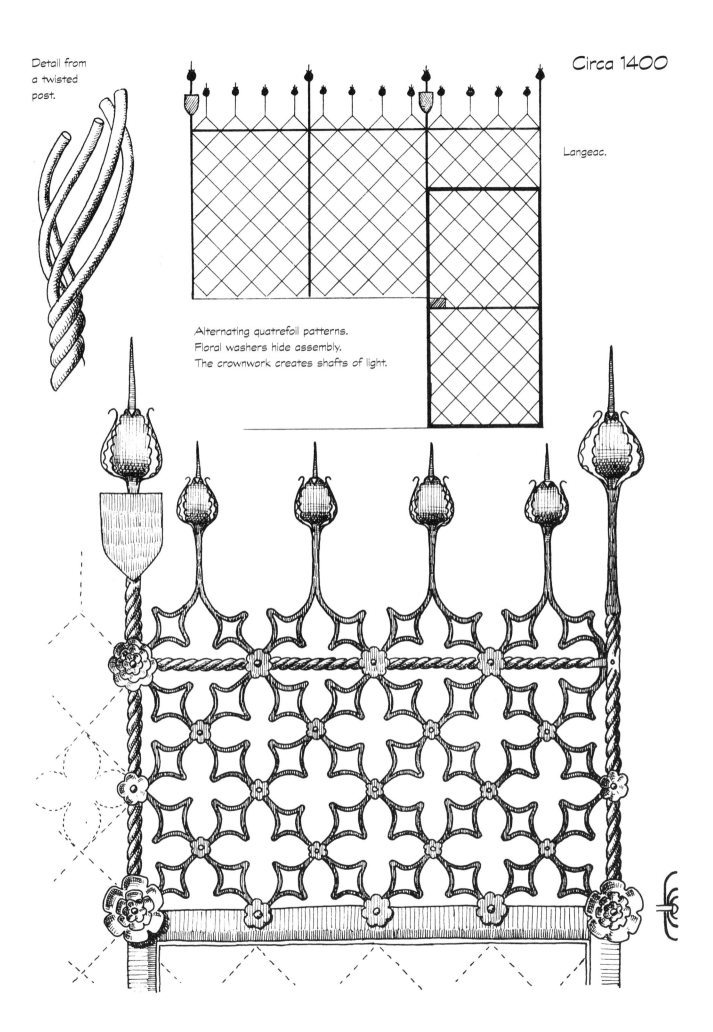

Detail from
a twisted
post.

Circa 1400

Langeac.

Alternating quatrefoil patterns.
Floral washers hide assembly.
The crownwork creates shafts of light.

14th century

Rouen. Musée Le Secq des Tournelles. Grille from the former cathedral screen.

Alternating patterns. Stamped ornaments. The lower section is decorated with fleur-de-lis, a motif used mostly at the time of Louis XIII.

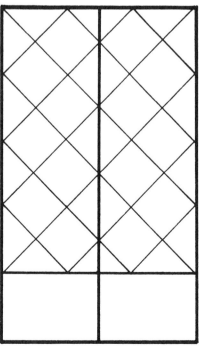

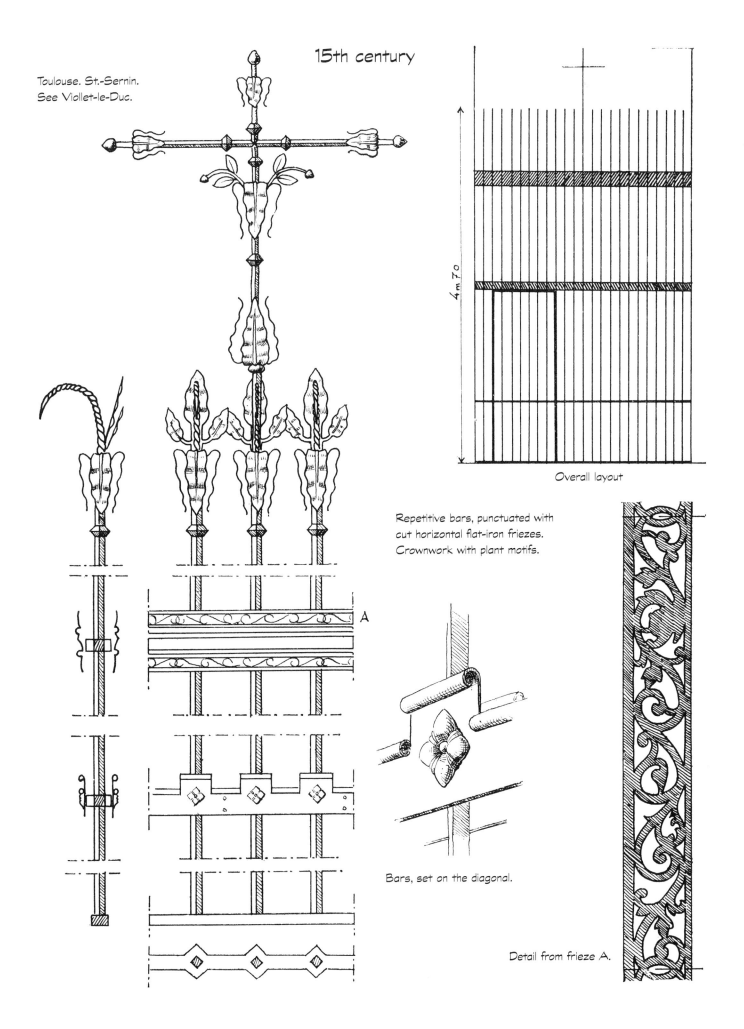

15th century

Toulouse. St.-Sernin.
See Viollet-le-Duc.

4m70

Overall layout

Repetitive bars, punctuated with
cut horizontal flat-iron friezes.
Crownwork with plant motifs.

A

Bars, set on the diagonal.

Detail from frieze A.

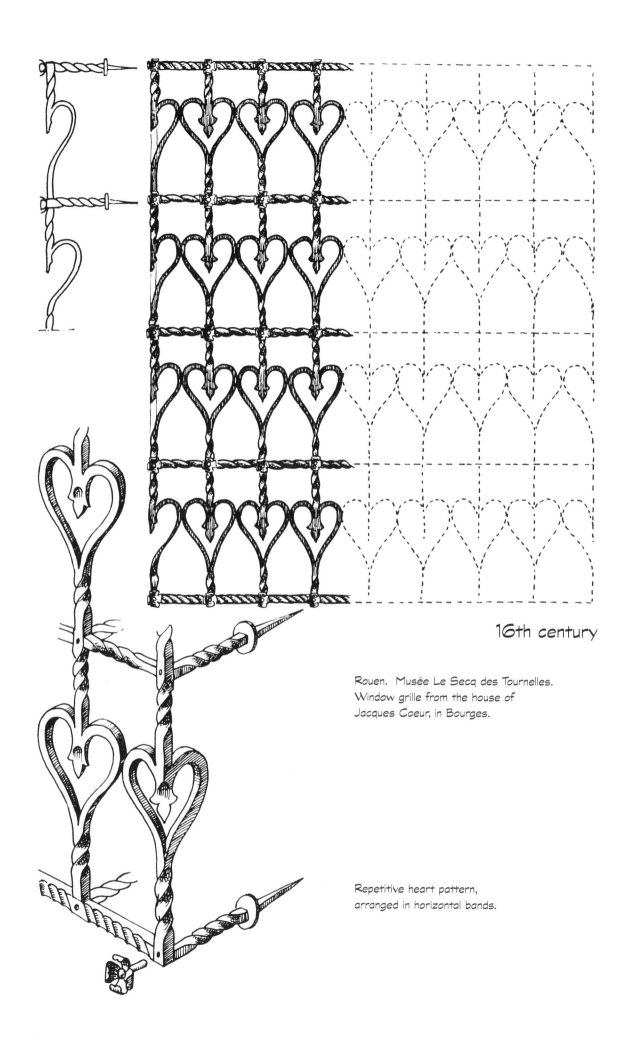

16th century

Rouen. Musée Le Secq des Tournelles.
Window grille from the house of
Jacques Coeur, in Bourges.

Repetitive heart pattern,
arranged in horizontal bands.

66

16th century

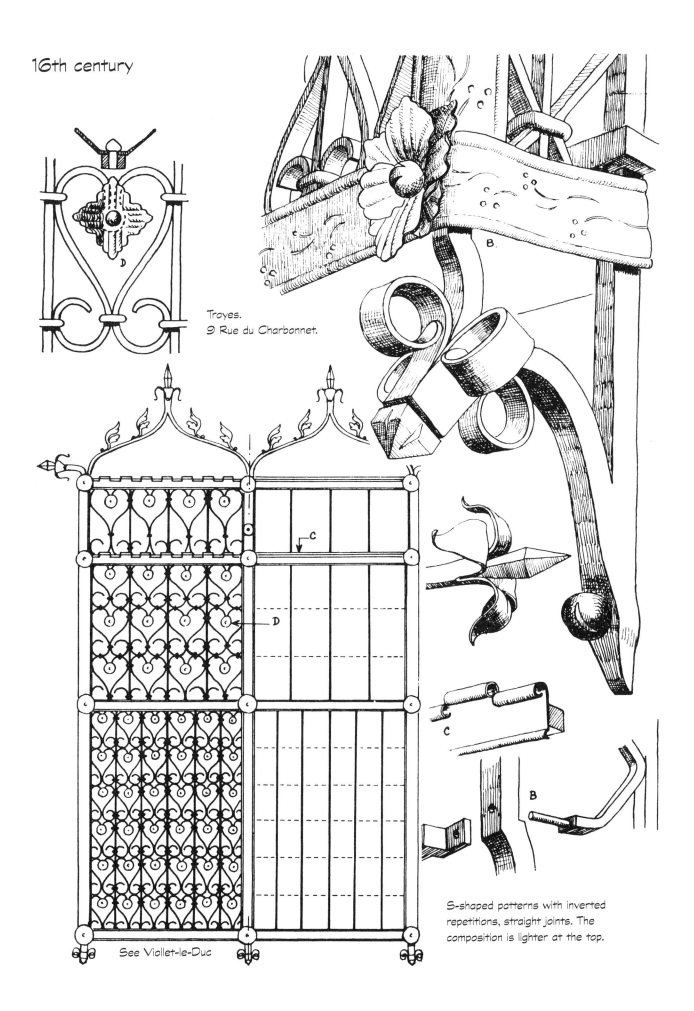

Troyes.
9 Rue du Charbonnet.

D

C

D

See Viollet-le-Duc

B.

C

B

S-shaped patterns with inverted
repetitions, straight joints. The
composition is lighter at the top.

Paris. Musée
Carnavalet.

A

Design in horizontal bands, inverted repetition of S-shape. Frame with repetition
of inverted C-shapes. Arched fanlight decorated with S-shapes.

68

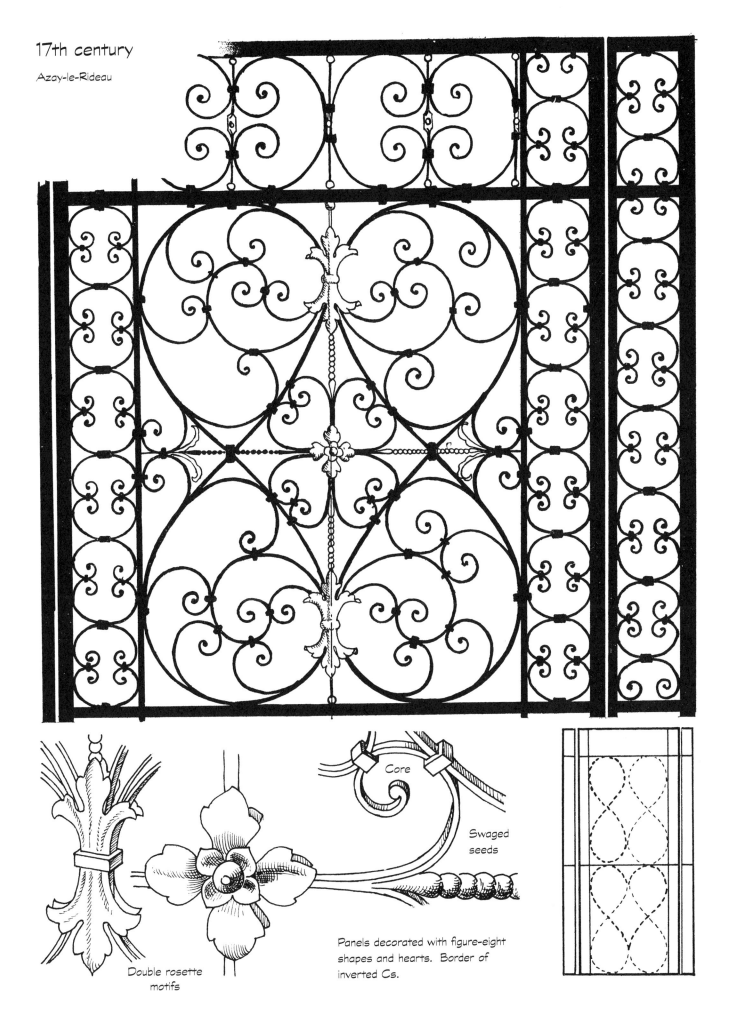

17th century

Azay-le-Rideau

Core

Swaged
seeds

Double rosette
motifs

Panels decorated with figure-eight
shapes and hearts. Border of
inverted Cs.

69

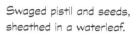

Swaged pistil and seeds,
sheathed in a waterleaf.

Azay-le-Rideau.

Protective grille.

Pattern in horizontal bands getting lighter toward the upper section.
The iron thins out progressively toward a rolled core.
Note how the collars are riveted in two places.

Pattern composed in panels topped with a horizontal frieze and crown.
The ensemble resembles embroidery.
The thin iron traces a light, open design that contrasts with foliage
groupings, executed in repoussé sheet metal.
This leafwork generally hides the assembly.

Tours. Eglise des Minimes.
See details page 29.

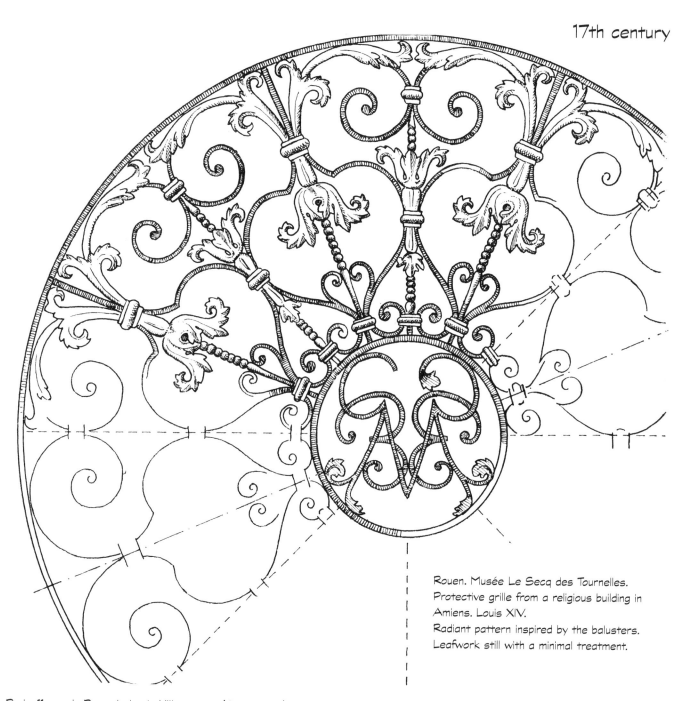

Rouen. Musée Le Secq des Tournelles.
Protective grille from a religious building in
Amiens. Louis XIV.
Radiant pattern inspired by the balusters.
Leafwork still with a minimal treatment.

Paris. 11 rue du Renard. Louis XIII transom (disappeared). Radiant pattern.

72

Paris. Lycée Henri IV. Louis XIV grille.

This design, laden with panels, creates a foundation for the composition. The bars, while enlivening the ensemble, let through light and view. The transom, lightly ornamented, doesn't outweigh the general decoration. The traced border solidly frames the whole piece. The leafwork only intervenes discreetly. The assembly uses half-lap joints.

Louis XV

Molded casing — Characteristic palm leaf

Amiens. Cathedral. Chapelle Notre-Dame de la Paix. 1768.

Paris. 27 quai de Béthune.

Nancy. Musée Historique Lorrain. Small interior grille. Asymmetrical design.

Louis XVI

76

Sées (Orne). Diocese.

The formal, prim design gives the impression of having been traced with a ruler, square, or compass.

Louis XVI

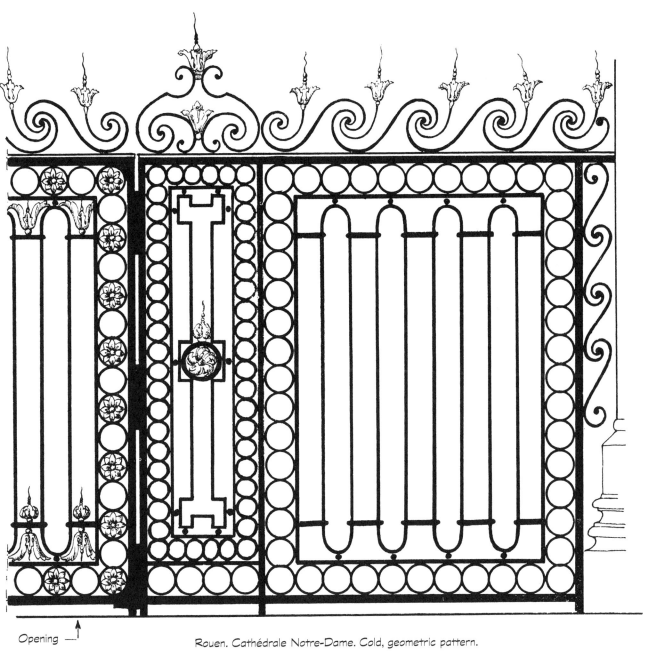

Rouen. Cathédrale Notre-Dame. Cold, geometric pattern.

Paris. St.-Roch. Communion railing.

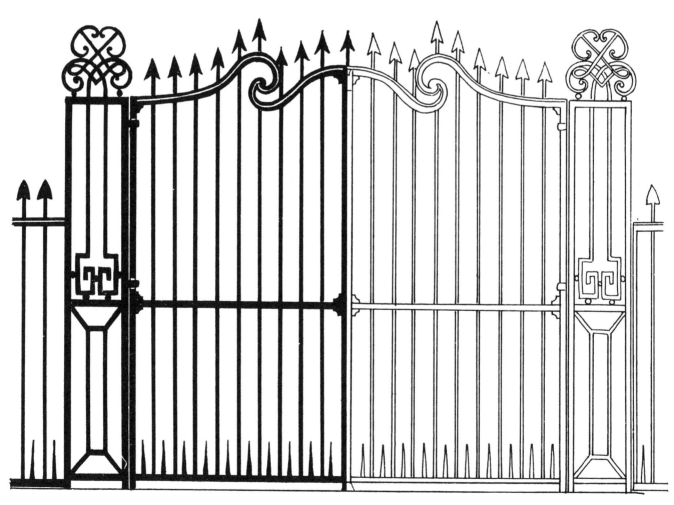

Château de la Rigaudière, near Le Theil (Ille-et-Vilaine), circa 1777.

Empire

The cast iron makes the decorative elements on this grille heavier.

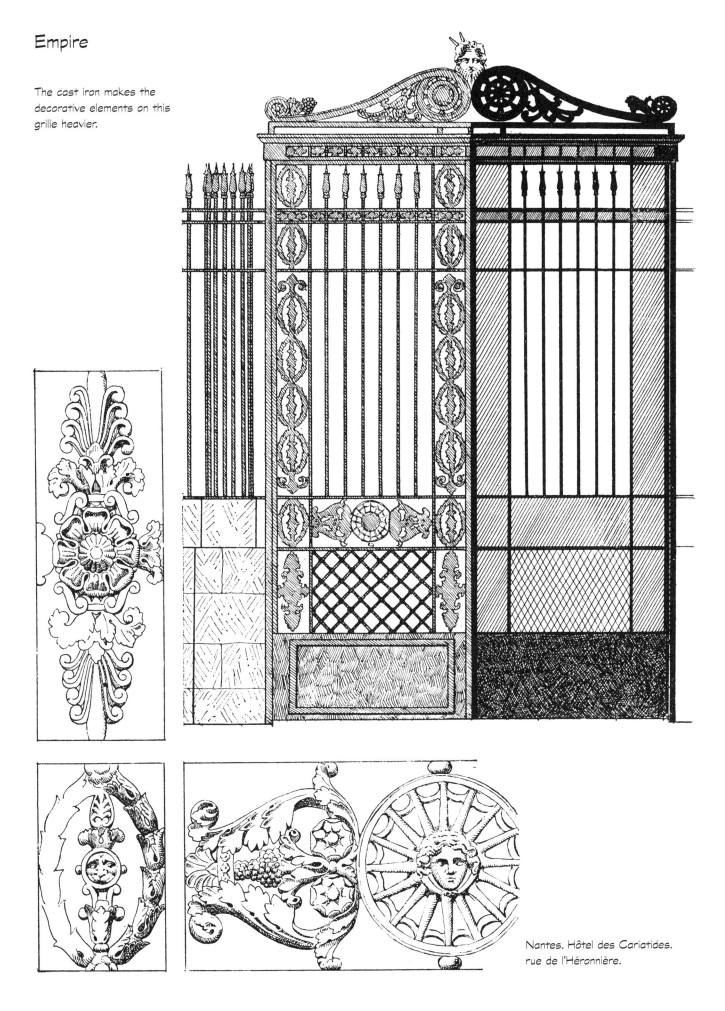

Nantes. Hôtel des Cariatides. rue de l'Héronnière.

Guardrails, Handrails, Balconies, Balustrades

Guardrails on windows had two functions: to provide support and prevent falls. To that end, their height must correspond to the average level of an adult's center of gravity, a minimum of 1 meter (3 feet) from the ground. The interior ironwork also must be sufficient to prevent anyone from passing through. As a result, the spaces must be equal to or less than 110 millimeters (4 inches).

Different Types

The size of the guardrails is a function of the height of the base; that is, the height from the ground to the top of the stone support (fig. 1).

HEIGHT OF BASE
a. 1 meter (3.3 feet) and more; protection unnecessary.
b. From 0.85 to 1 meter (2.8 and 3.3 feet); a support bar with a single crosspiece with no sharp angles on top.
c. From 0.75 to 0.85 meters (2.5 to 2.8 feet); a cross support with several crosspieces or a single crosspiece with a decorative pattern.
d. From 0.35 to 0.75 meters (1.1 to 2.5 feet); a small balcony with two crosspieces held together by two posts and an interior decorative pattern.
e. Less than 0.35 meters (1.1 feet); balcony, with two crosspieces plus two posts set into the stone base.

Balcony

A balcony is a platform of varying width, projecting out from a façade, supported by brackets or columns. This platform, placed into an opening (door or window), allows for standing. It is surrounded by a protective railing executed in wood, stone, or metal.

PRINCIPAL ELEMENTS (fig. 4)
A. Corner posts set back from the platform edge: 90 millimeters (3.5 inches) minimum.
B. Upper horizontal in which to insert the handrail.
C. Lower horizontal in three pieces attached to the corner posts with brazed, pinned dowels (fig. 5). These bars are set into the façade: 100 millimeters (4 inches) minimum.
D. Infill.

Guardrail

Placed at leaning height along a gallery or terrace, a guardrail is meant to prevent falls. Guardrails are a basic construction and only have posts and crosspieces and sometimes diagonals.

INSTALLATION
This depends on shutter placement and the size of the stone sill.
a. Shutters or louvered shutters folding toward the façade: Guardrails placed into the setting (fig. 2). Length of the setting: crosspieces, 50 to 100 millimeters (2 to 4 inches) depending on the material; handrail inserted 20 millimeters (0.8 inches). Plan for a > b and c > 2b.
b. Louvered shutters folding into the setting (fig. 3). Guardrails set into the façade. The crosspieces forming bands are angled; the settings or anchoring pieces are bent outward slightly into the masonry.
a. 50 to 80 millimeters (2 to 3 inches) minimum.
b. 80 to 100 millimeters (3 to 4 inches) minimum.

Balustrade

A guardrail becomes a balustrade when the spaces within the infill are less than 100 millimeters (4 inches).

A corbel on the façade of a building, a balustrade becomes a large balcony that allows for standing or for passing from one entry to another (fig. 6).

PRINCIPAL ELEMENTS
The girder, from 1.5 to 2 meters (4.9 to 6.6 feet), is brought together by posts with U-shaped buttresses, sometimes cut and set into the thickness of the platform (fig. 7). This girder may be divided by pilasters with buttressed posts.

Code

In France, facing neighboring property, cloistered or not, balconies and other projections must maintain 19 decameters (1.9 meters or 6.2 feet) between the wall where they are to be placed and the neighboring property. This distance must be measured from the exterior edge of the balcony (or other projection) to the point where the neighboring property begins (Civil code, art. 678 and 680).

For balconies facing public spaces, construction rights are based on specific rulings; municipal councils grant requests based on visual and zoning considerations.

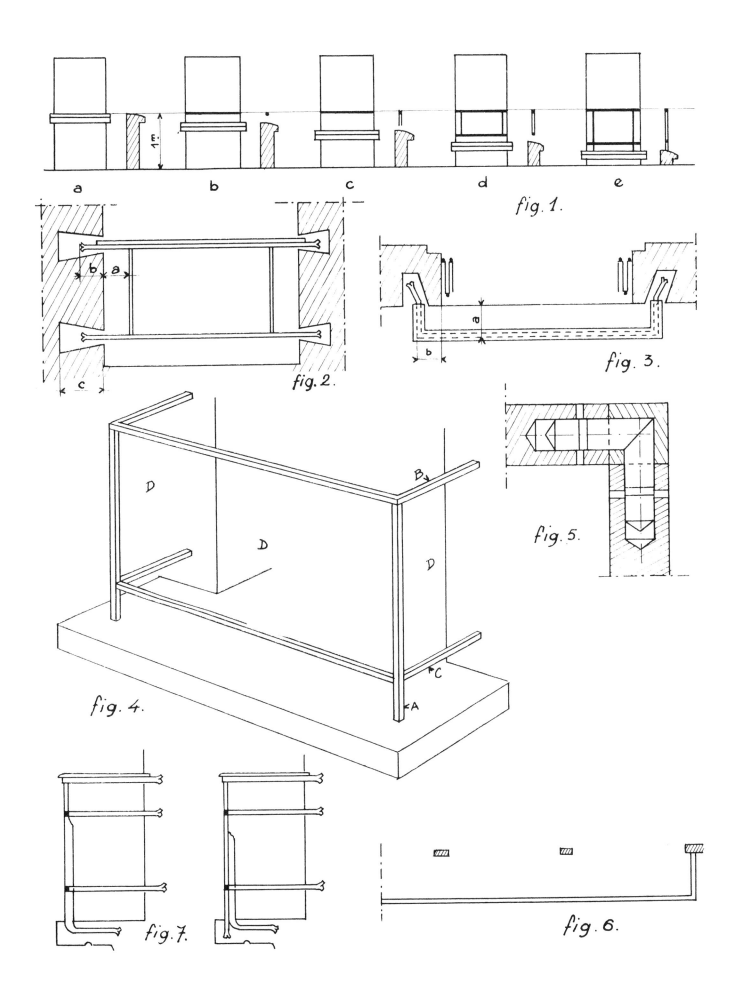

fig. 1.

fig. 2.

fig. 3.

fig. 4.

fig. 5.

fig. 6.

fig. 7.

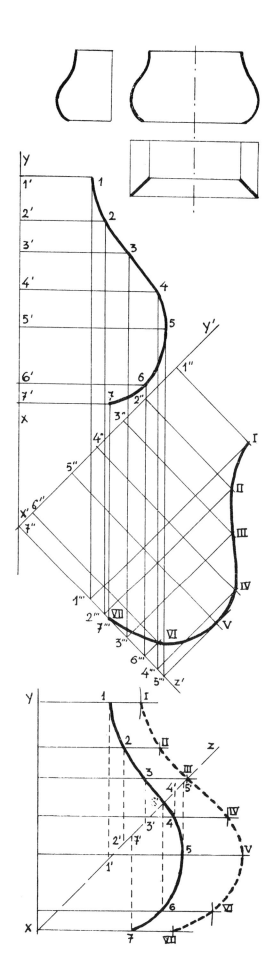

Curved Balconies

Curved, or basket, balconies are characteristic of Louis XV style. The line for the corner posts, or edges, and that of design presents certain difficulties.

I. Outline of the Edge

THEORY

a) A certain number of points are placed along the exact profile of the balcony: 1, 2, 3, etc.

b) These points are carried out horizontally on a vertical X/Y axis, as 1', 2', 3', etc.

c) A right angle X'Y' and X'Z' is drawn, and rotated 45°, along the vertical X/Y axis.

d) On the axis X'Y', the distances 1', 2', 3', etc., become 1", 2", 3", etc.

e) A line is drawn vertically from points 1, 2, 3, etc., to the line X'Z' to find 1"', 2"', 3"', etc.

f) At the intersection of the perpendiculars extended to line X'Y' from points 1", 2", 3", and of the perpendiculars extended to line X'Z' from points 1"', 2"', 3"', we obtain points I, II, III, etc., which determine the exact curve of the edge.

PRACTICAL LAYOUT

The ironsmith employs a method that avoids using too large a sheet metal and the drawing of long parallels.
A 45° angle is created directly from line XY, to make XZ, for example (most often within the design itself). The points 1, 2, 3, etc. are dropped down from this line. With a compass, the distances X1', X2', etc., are determined from XY on the horizontal lines passing through points 1, 2, 3, etc., in order to obtain points I, II, III, etc., by which the contour of the edge post is determined.

II. Outline of the Decoration

DEVELOPMENT OF THE FORM

A. Elevation of the balcony.

B. Development.

   a) A certain number of points are determined along an exact profile: 1, 2, 3, etc.
   b) The distances are marked between 1-2, 2-3, etc., on the line X'Y' to create 1', 2', 3', etc.
   c) At the intersection of verticals drawn from 1, 2, 3, and from horizontals drawn from 1', 2', 3', the points I, II, III, etc. are obtained to determine the balcony's curvature.

It is upon the resulting outline that the ironsmith can work out the design to true scale.

CONTROLLING CURVED FORMS

The ironsmith forms a thin piece of sheet metal behind the framework of the posts and horizontals, so it takes on the desired curves; the exact outline of the decoration is drawn onto the sheet metal. In this way, the forging work and the bending of the pattern can be controlled.

For a curved balcony that is raised up and seen from above, it is desirable to create a plaster mold onto which the design is transferred, and then adjust the various elements of the ensemble. Once the assembly is finished, the plaster template is broken. If the same model is to be reproduced several times, a removable template is made.

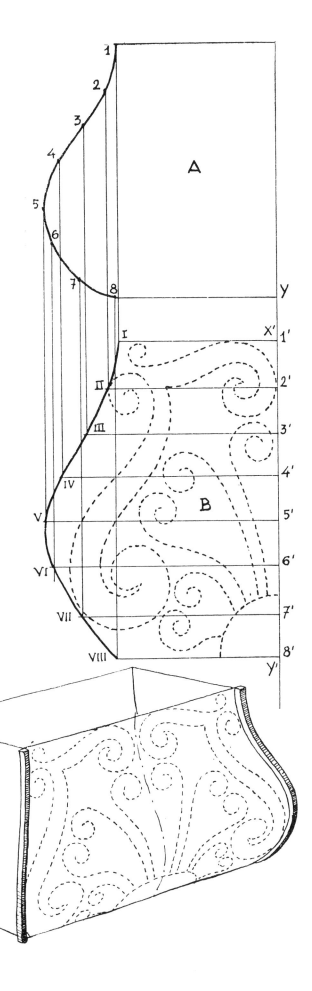

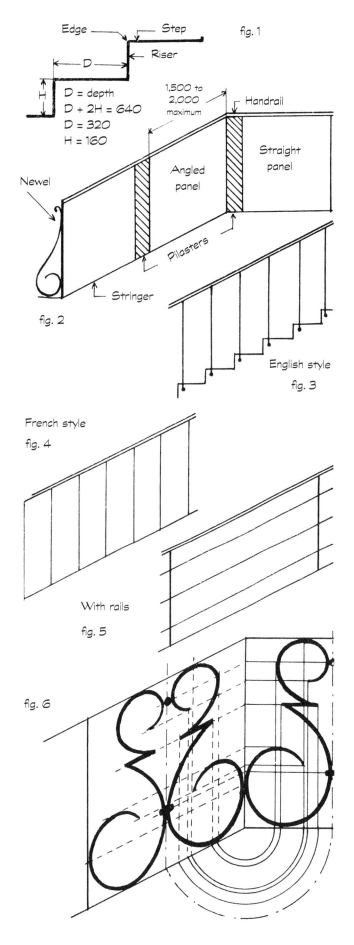

Edge — Step — fig. 1

Riser

D

H

D = depth
D + 2H = 640
D = 320
H = 160

1,500 to
2,000 maximum

Handrail

Straight
panel

Angled
panel

Newel

Pilasters

Stringer

fig. 2

English style
fig. 3

French style
fig. 4

With rails
fig. 5

fig. 6

Handrails

Handrails, which can be made from various materials such as wood, stone, or iron, are designed to prevent falls and facilitate ascending or descending the stairs. Handrails must be quite stable and able to withstand both pushing and leaning. In order to provide sufficient protection, the spaces between the posts, crosspieces, and designs must not exceed 110 millimeters (4.3 inches), and the minimum height of the handrail must be 1,000 millimeters (39 inches), measured from the edge of the step.

PRINCIPAL ELEMENTS

Fig. 2 shows the different parts of a handrail: posts, pilasters (if there are any), secondary rails (depending on the design: see fig. 5), straight and angled panels, newel, and railing.

DIFFERENT TYPES

Usually, handrails are distinguished as:

• English style, attached on the exterior (fig. 3);
• French style, attached on the stringer (fig. 4);
• with rails (fig. 5);
• with panels (fig. 2).

DESIGN

The design of handrails is, in principle, based on repetition and composed of a series of panels, except for a few examples of Louis XV style. These panels may be separated by pilasters (fig. 2).

Patterns undergo some alterations when it comes to sloping panels (fig. 6). These alterations are important in curved sections. In addition, the division of horizontal parts doesn't always correspond to that of the sloping parts.

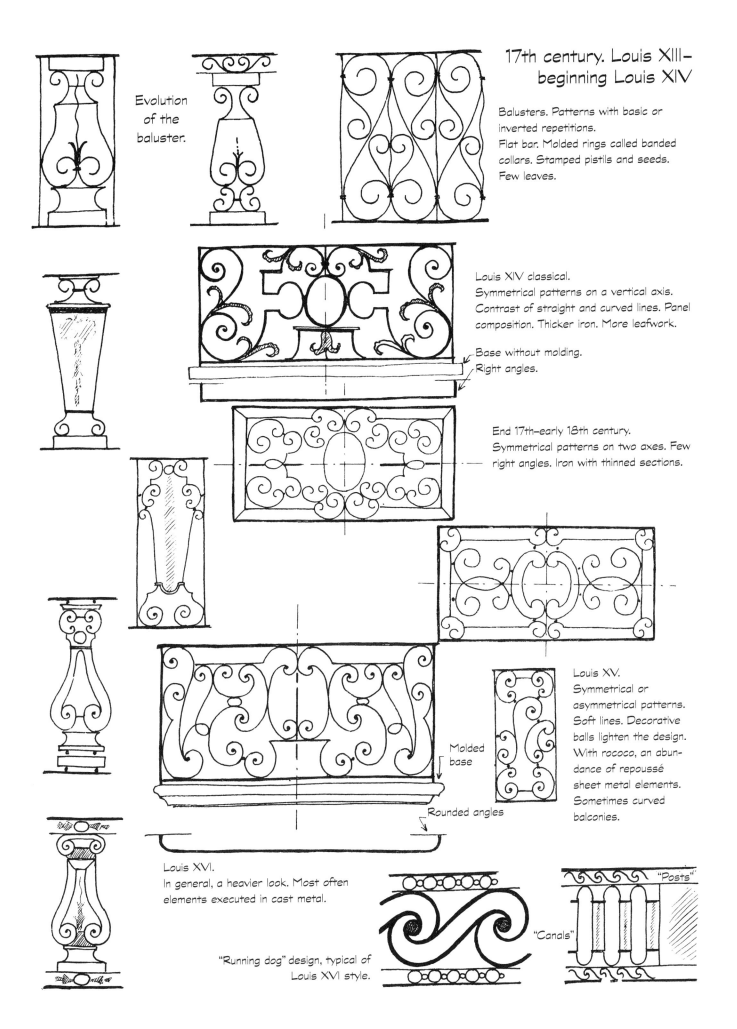

Evolution of the baluster.

17th century. Louis XIII– beginning Louis XIV

Balusters. Patterns with basic or inverted repetitions.
Flat bar. Molded rings called banded collars. Stamped pistils and seeds. Few leaves.

Louis XIV classical.
Symmetrical patterns on a vertical axis. Contrast of straight and curved lines. Panel composition. Thicker iron. More leafwork.

Base without molding.
Right angles.

End 17th–early 18th century.
Symmetrical patterns on two axes. Few right angles. Iron with thinned sections.

Louis XV.
Symmetrical or asymmetrical patterns. Soft lines. Decorative balls lighten the design. With rococo, an abundance of repoussé sheet metal elements. Sometimes curved balconies.

Molded base

Rounded angles

Louis XVI.
In general, a heavier look. Most often elements executed in cast metal.

"Running dog" design, typical of Louis XVI style.

"Canals"

"Posts"

85

History of Railings and Balconies

The oldest known balcony in France is the chassis said to be of Charles IX, on display at the Louvre. The original fragments (sixteenth century) are still numerous despite the important restorations made in the nineteenth century.

Wrought-iron balconies and railings did not come into vogue in architectural ornamentation until the seventeenth century, under Louis XIII. Often conceived together, they follow a similar evolution of form.

The usual type is based on the baluster, with or without frieze, and on the heart-shaping S. These patterns are in basic repetition in the case of balusters, and inverted for S-shapes. Carried out in flat iron, they have very few elements in sheet metal. A few parts are stamped—collars and pistils—to catch the light.

The balconies in the private homes in Lauzun and on Rue Bretonvilliers, or the railing in the Hôtel Salé in Paris, demonstrate the survival of this type of composition under Louis XIV. Symmetrical compositions with one or two axes mark the classical period; large panels are alternated with smaller panels or pilasters. C-, S-, and X-shapes or shapes like the number 3 often form the pattern, and straight lines contrast with curves. The iron becomes heavier and pressed sheet metal comes into wider use: infill wins out over empty space as time progresses, as witnessed by the railings of the Grand Trianon.

Even though it follows the tradition of Louis XIV style, Louis XV style at its beginning is distinguished by gentler lines, ornamental balls, and leafwork silhouettes. This last element is often executed in bronze or cast iron when the patterns are repeated. Curved lines exist not only in the pattern but also in the framework, particularly in stairway handrails and balcony bases, which had been straight during the seventeenth century.

The design, often asymmetrical, is characteristic of the rococo period. The stairway railings at Hôtel de Ville in Nancy, created by Jean Lamour, are a fine example of this. Louis XVI style, which picks up on older formulas, is often difficult to define, except for its cold, heavy character (as with grillework) and the use of cast iron elements preferably in sheet metal repoussé. Frequent patterns during this period are S-shapes, fluting, and Greek designs.

RAILING BASE

The bases of stair railings reflect different styles. Four pilasters forming a square casing, topped with a brass ball, compose the common base under Louis XIII.

The newel is embellished with the form of an S-shaped console under Louis XIV, a design that remains with a couple of variants throughout the eighteenth century. The base of the stairway is always horizontal and the railing is always at a right angle.

The curved line triumphs with Louis XV. The foot conserves its console theme but is embellished with curves and countercurves. A cast bronze vase replaces the brass ball. The base of the stairway has a slanted curve to it, and the railing has a curved base; often, staircases double back at the landing.

Under Louis XVI, the base again takes on the character it had under Louis XIV. The S-shape becomes larger, thereby increasing the size of the scrolls, which are decorated with rosettes. The base is sometimes made up of straight casings in a square shape, as exhibited on the railing of the Palais-Royal, Paris.

17th century

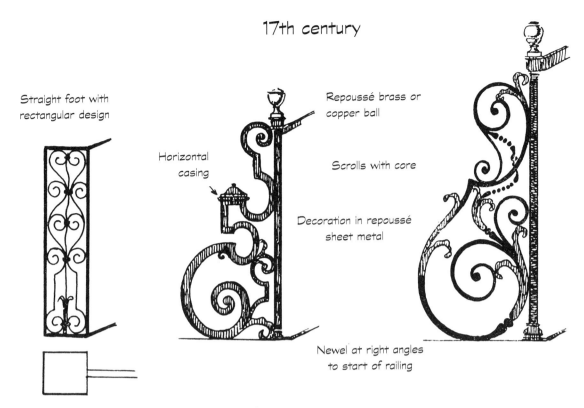

Straight foot with rectangular design

Horizontal casing

Repoussé brass or copper ball

Scrolls with core

Decoration in repoussé sheet metal

Newel at right angles to start of railing

18th century

Louis XV

Louis XVI

Scrolls: protruding core or ram's horn

S-shaped casing

Cast-iron vase

Garlands

Decoration: cast iron, little sheet metal

Greek style

Decoration: repoussé sheet metal and cast metal

← Newel angled and curved with stairway →

Few or no right angles

← Curved angles
Twisting staircases are common →

Paris. Rue Bretonvilliers.

These two balconies, though dating from the Louis XIV period, still borrow elements from Louis XIII style: slimness of iron bars, precision of leaf contouring.

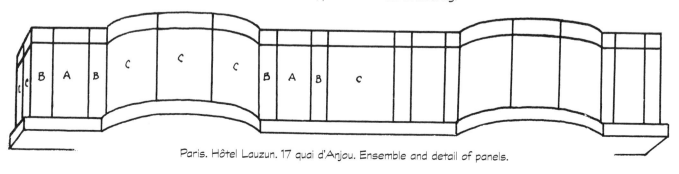

Paris. Hôtel Lauzun. 17 quai d'Anjou. Ensemble and detail of panels.

Paris. 42 rue de Turenne.

Paris. Lycée Charlemagne.

Versailles. Grand Trianon.
Railing designed and executed by
Fordrin, circa 1688.
See details pp. 30 and 31.

Balusters with square
end casings.

Characteristic garland

Louis XIV

Left. Paris.
Hôtel d'Argouges.
16 rue Séguier.

Right. Nantes.
Hôtel Becdelièvre.
13 rue Briard.

Louis XV

Paris. Hôtel d'Ecquevilly. Called "the
Huntsman." Railing with hunting ornamentation recalling the huntsman's
activities.

Paris. Hôtel de Marcilly.
18 rue du Cherche-Midi.
See railing p. 95.

This newel, in rococo style, is without a doubt
unique in its type.

Paris. Hôtel de Suistel.
52 rue de Vaugirard.

Nantes. Hôtel d'Aux.
2 place du Maréchal Foch.

Paris. 88 rue Bonaparte.

The central palm leaf spreads and blends with
the rest of the design.

Louis XV

Paris. Hôtel d'Ecquevilly.
60 rue de Turenne.

Paris. 13 rue du Regard.

Railing bases. Soft lines,
no straight lines.

Nantes. 1 rue Tournefort.

94

Palm leaves

1.

1. and 3. Paris. Hôtel de
Marcilly. See newel p. 92.
Asymmetrical design.

2. and 4. Paris. Former convent
of English Benedictines.
269 rue St. Jacques.
2. Railing with asymmetrical
design.
4. Balcony, Louis XIV style
persists.

2.

3.

4.

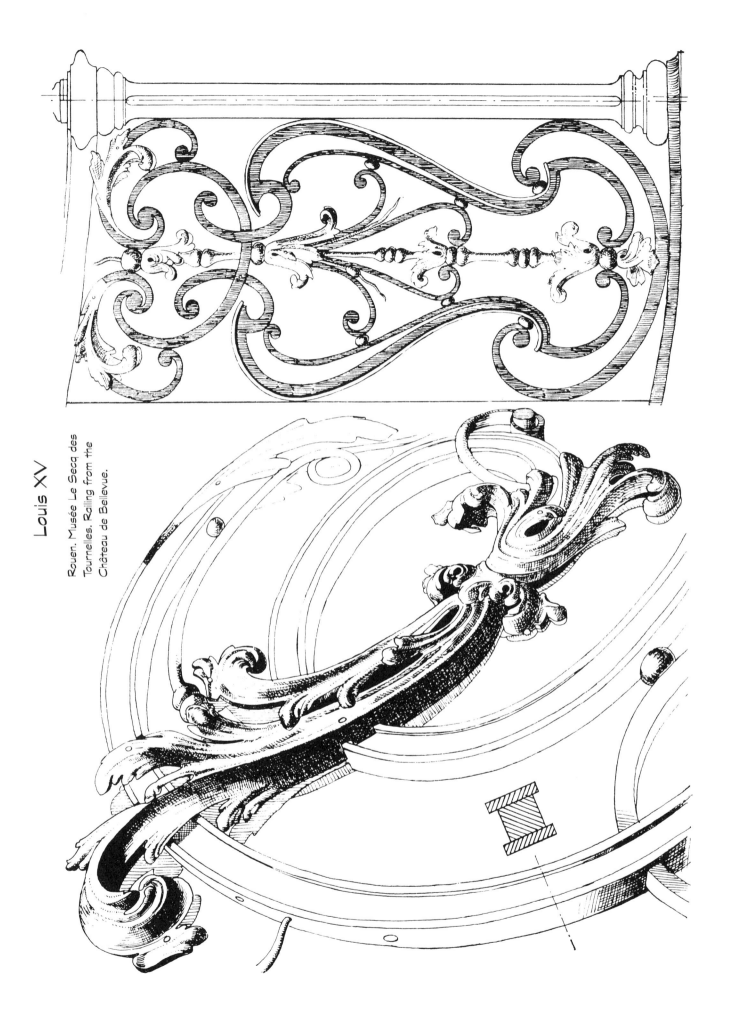

Louis XV

Rouen. Musée Le Secq des
Tournelles. Railing from the
Château de Bellevue.

Louis XV

Paris. 27 rue St.-André-des-Arts.

Nantes. Musée du Château.

97

Top: Versailles. 8 rue St.-Louis.

Middle: Paris. 6 Place St.-Sulpice.

Bottom: Montauban. Cathedral.

Louis XV

Top: Paris. 44 rue St.-André-des-Arts.

Middle: Pezenas. 9 rue Victor Hugo.

Bottom: Montauban. Cathedral.

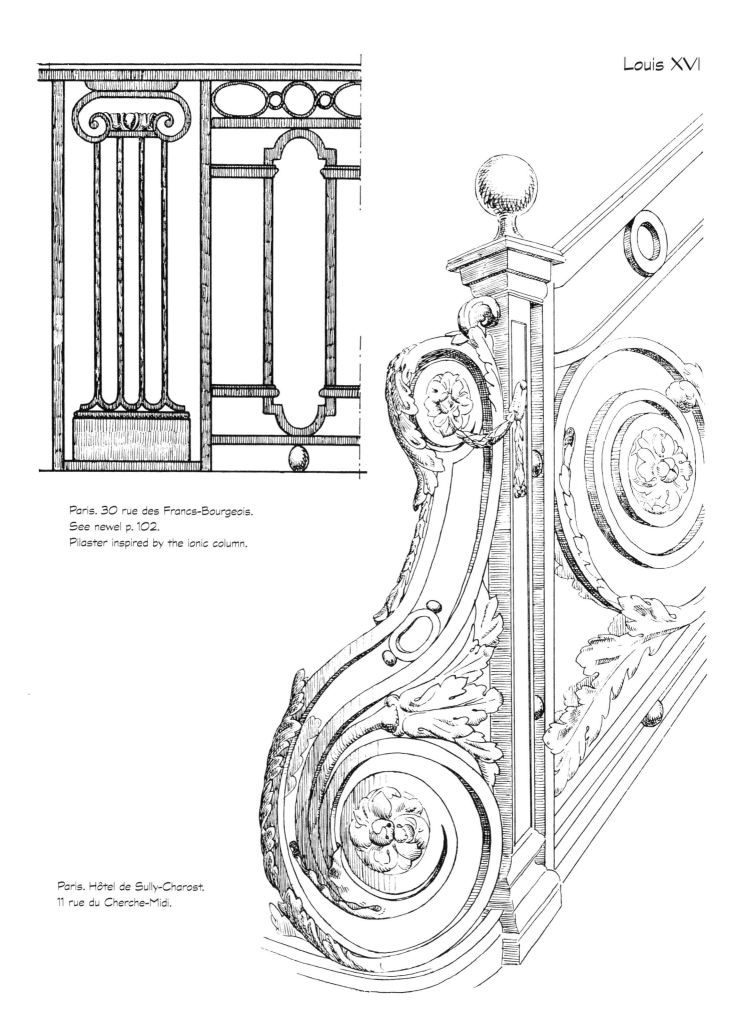

Paris. 30 rue des Francs-Bourgeois.
See newel p. 102.
Pilaster inspired by the ionic column.

Paris. Hôtel de Sully-Charost.
11 rue du Cherche-Midi.

Louis XVI

Right: Paris. 127 rue de Grenelle.
Baluster with ionic capital.

Left: Paris. 58 rue du Faubourg-Poissonière.

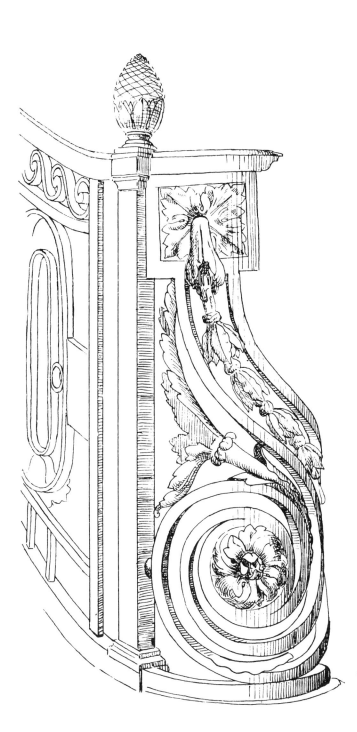

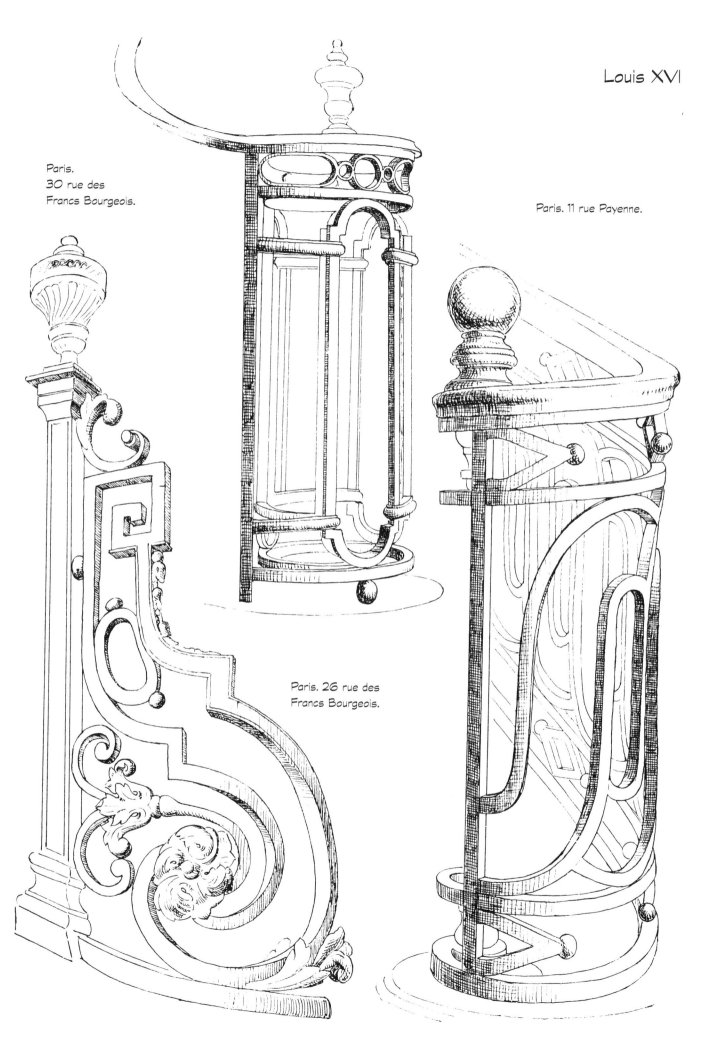

Paris.
30 rue des
Francs Bourgeois.

Paris. 11 rue Payenne.

Paris. 26 rue des
Francs Bourgeois.

Locks

The French term *serrure* comes from the Latin *sera*, which refers to a portable lock or padlock. It is similar to the French verb *serrer*, to grip or tighten.

Worried about their own security, as well as the security of their belongings, people have always made an effort to protect their homes. They partially resolved this problem with the bolt (a wood or iron bar) held by tracks fixed onto the panel of a door and locked into a cavity built into the frame. But this type of lock was only useful from inside the home. In order to maneuver it from the outside, it needed to be complemented with a key. This was, in the beginning, just a simple hook inserted through the door, which pushed the bolt to the desired position. This rudimentary system, quite easy to pick, offered little guarantee of security.

Locks that work with linear movement of the key

In security locks used by the Egyptians, movable pins were inserted in the bolt to maneuver it. The height of the bolt equaled the height to which the pins had to be raised to make the bolt slide. The end of the key was fitted with the specific lugs. The key, sliding horizontally, dragged the bolt and locked it into the keeper (fig. 1).

The Romans, then the Gallo-Romans, held to the same principle. The teeth on their keys were irregularly cut along a curved line (fig. 2). The key in fig. 3 has, at a right angle to the lugs or prongs, a pierced square bit; these prongs hooked into the fittings placed under the bolt.

The key fittings shown in fig. 4 are carved out: they were inserted into the corresponding hollow openings in the bolt; one of them lifted the end of a spring that kept the bolt in its locked position.

Locks that work with a partial turn of the key

From the twelfth to seventeenth centuries, locks with partial rotations were used. They worked only from the outside (fig. 5).

The lock's case was carved into the wood of the door; one of the sides held the fittings.

The entry (A), cut into the outside plate, was horizontal. The end of the key shaft was inserted into a socket (B), which helped to guide the key and prevented it from going in too far. The holes in the bit slid over the fittings (D), which were fixed into the box. Upon rotating, the front edge of the bit fitted with three notches (D), pushed a spring (E), thanks to notches located on the edge of the bit, disengaged a stop (F) that was fixed in place under the bolt (G), and moved the bolt.

To remove the key, it was necessary to turn the lock back.

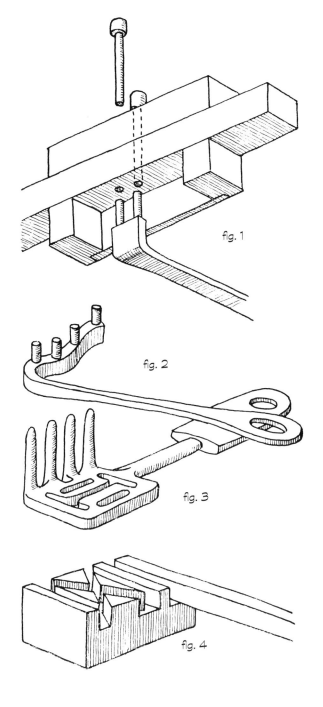

fig. 1

fig. 2

fig. 3

fig. 4

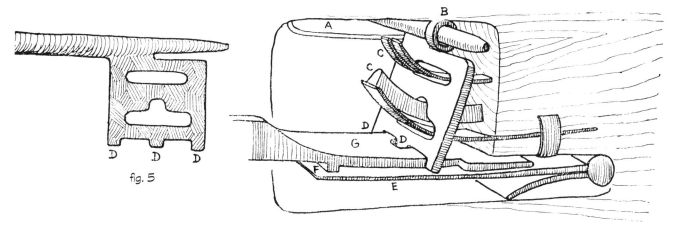

fig. 5

We will not look at special locks here, such as the Bramah lock, perfected by the Englishman Bramah in the beginning of the nineteenth century, or the Yale lock, inspired by the Egyptian pin locks.

Locks that work with a full turn of the key

These locks, like the preceding ones, function by temporarily immobilizing certain opening elements. The mechanism is moved with a key making a full turn—this is the case with the dead lock—or with a button if the lock is a half-turn bolt. The double-bolt lock, used from the seventeenth century, combines the two systems.

A lock (fig. 6) is made up of a box or case that contains the functioning parts called wards, which are fixed onto a lock plate. The outside of the lock plate is penetrated by the key hole and, possibly, by a circular hole to allow a slide bolt.

Along with the lock plate, the case has three other partition plates and a head plate, drilled to allow for the passage of one or more bolts. A non-removable fitting plate completes the ensemble, closing up the box with screws that fix into stop pins, square shafts fixed to the lock plate. The fitting plate has an exterior tube that passes through the wood of the door and directs the key. A tube may also be found within the box to guide a piped key and help it rotate.

A lock functions by allowing a bolt slide to engage it or disengage it in a keeper affixed to the doorframe. The key, when it turns, raises a tumbler that a spring holds in place; it frees the bolt stop held in the notches on the top of the bolt (figs. 7 and 8). As it turns, the key moves the barbs and pushes the bolt forward or backward (fig. 9). This displacement provides only relative security; locks of this type are easy to pick. To guarantee efficient locking, it is important that a lock work only with a specific key.

All modern locks are derived from two main types. In the first, the fittings, more or less complex, prevent any key with the wrong fittings or openings from entering or working. The term *fitting* designates the plate that gets fixed onto the lock plate with posts and holds the key slot, the riveted wards on the partition, the wards, and the escutcheons held onto the lock plate and the fitting plate (fig. 10).

The second type of lock is characterized by a series of tumblers. Locks with multiple tumblers, called tumbler locks, were invented about 1820 by an Englishman named Schub.

When the key is turned, each tumbler is raised to a different height in order to line up with a tab or tumbler post when the bolt passes. Affixed to the bolt, this catch replaces the bolt stop (fig. 11).

A pin key, used from either side of the lock, always consists of an even number of tumblers. The ridges in the key are aligned symmetrically along the length of the bit (fig. 12).

With piped keys, the number of tumblers and ridges is variable. In certain cases, tumblers and fittings are combined.

The piped key, designed to increase lock security, is an improvement born in the fifteenth century. The shaft is pierced with a triangle, a heart, a cloverleaf, or a fleur-de-lis. A round tube carved to the form of the piece attached to the fitting plate allows the key to rotate (fig. 14).

In the eighteenth century, the bits were shaped to form letters or numbers (fig. 13); the keyhole had a corresponding design.

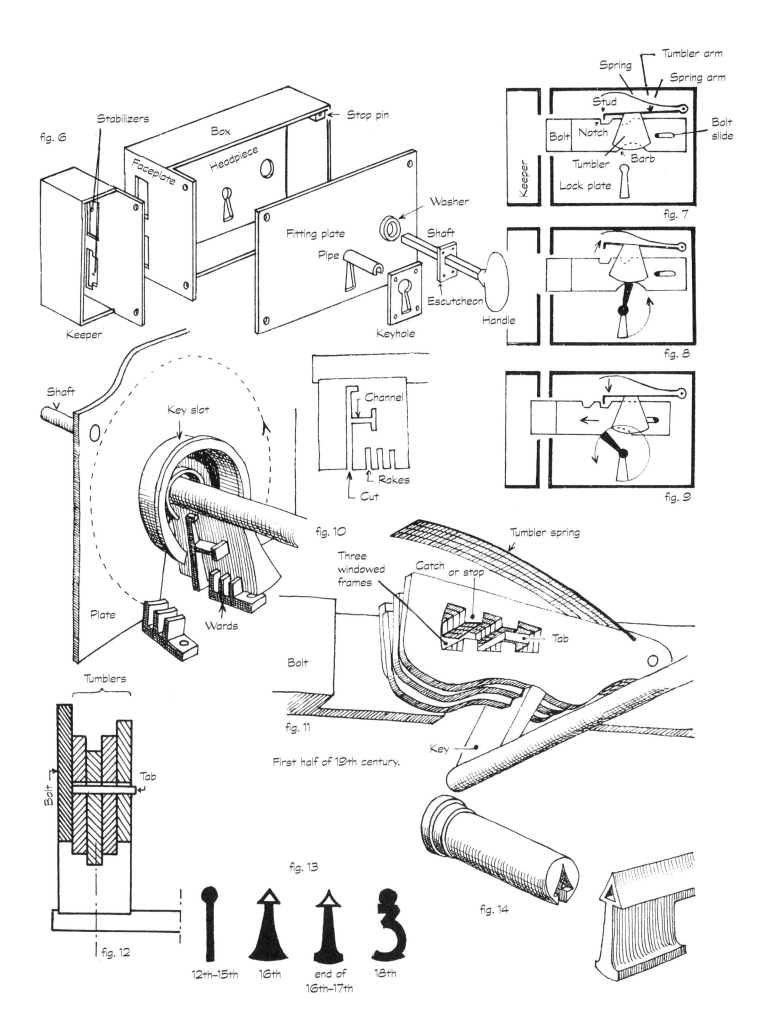

fig. 6

Stabilizers

Box

Stop pin

Faceplate

Headpiece

Fitting plate

Washer

Shaft

Pipe

Escutcheon

Handle

Keeper

Keyhole

Spring

Tumbler arm

Spring arm

Stud

Bolt

Notch

Bolt slide

Keeper

Tumbler

Barb

Lock plate

fig. 7

fig. 8

Shaft

Key slot

Channel

fig. 9

Rakes

Cut

fig. 10

Plate

Wards

Tumbler spring

Three windowed frames

Catch or stop

Tab

Bolt

Key

Tumblers

First half of 19th century.

Bolt

Tab

fig. 11

fig. 13

fig. 12

12th–15th   16th   end of 16th–17th   18th

fig. 14

105

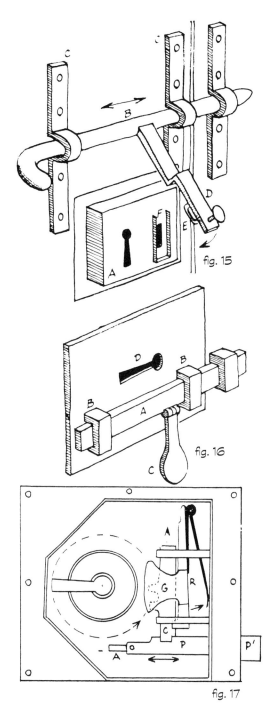

fig. 15

fig. 16

fig. 17

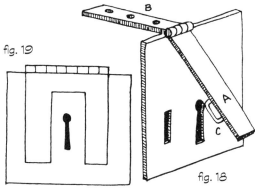

fig. 19

fig. 18

External lock

Looking at fig. 15, you can see:

- the box (A), made from a plate in repoussé;
- the bolt (B), sliding through the bolt-staples (C), attached above and independent of the lock.

Its movement is limited by the latch (D), holding the hasp, which shuts into the lock. The end of the bar is fitted with a latch (E), which slides into the keeper (F) cut into the lock box. The lock bolt slides into the catch. The system is similar to those described in figs. 7, 8, and 9.

This type of lock was still in use in the seventeenth century; Perpignan's city hall is home to a lock of this style that dates from 1693.

Locks with bolt-staples

In French, these are called either *serrures à verterelles* or *à vertenelles*. These names come from the Latin *verticula*, which means vertebra.

The lock casing is fitted into the wood of the door (fig. 16).

The bolt (A) protrudes from the lock plate and slides through the bolt-staples (B). The key does not move the bolt, rather the bolt is moved by hand with the help of a *pendant* or *ballotière* (C). The keyhole (D) is always horizontal.

By looking at how the mechanisms function (fig. 17), you can see that the interior bolt (P) is riveted to the exterior bolt (P'). The rivets glide along a runner (A), pierced through the lock plate and limiting the bolt's range of movement. The interior bolt is stuck in the locked position by a stop (C). To disengage it, a turn of the key pushes against a tumbler (G) held by a spring (R), which pushes the stop up, allowing the bolt to be moved.

Most often, the lock is double-sided, and the fitting plate and lock plate are similarly decorated.

Another ballotière riveted to the interior bolt allows for the opening and closing of the lock, on the fitting plate.

The bolt-staple lock disappeared around the fifteenth century.

Clasp locks

The clasp lock (fig. 18) is used for locking safe boxes. It functions like the external lock, but its case is built in. The hasp (A) moves on a hinge plate (B) connected to the cover of the box. On the inside of the end of the latch, a clasp (C) inserts into the keeper and is held by the bolt. Locking may be automatic with the help of a catch that hooks into the clasp, but opening must always be done with the key. In the beginning, the clasp latch was not centered on the lock plate, which made the lock mechanism simpler. As it evolved, double latches were designed in order to create an overall symmetry (fig. 19).

In the fifteenth and sixteenth centuries, mainly, a decorated plate hid the keyhole. The keyhole cover could be moved by pressing on one of the decorative elements.

Architecture often inspired the design of double-sided bolt-staple locks: fitting plates and lock plates, and the design of clasp locks with alternating orbe-voie arcading and pinnacles with people and animals sculpted in the round. At the end of the fifteenth century, the bottom edges were chisel cut with designs similar to thistles.

In the sixteenth century, the abundance of sculpture and moldings led locksmiths to invent smaller locks. The box was assembled, as in carpentry, with tenons, mortises, and dovetails. The shape of key piping, the fixtures, and even the mechanism became increasingly complicated. Open-work ornamentation continued but it was no longer ribbed. Lightly contoured clovers, vines, and thistles appeared on lock cases created during the reign of Louis XII.

These works mark the transition between Gothic and Renaissance styles.

The reign of François I witnessed the abandonment of cut-out designs in favor of repoussé, whose importance grew throughout the sixteenth century and the beginning of the seventeenth century. Imitating antiquity, chimeras, grotesque heads, and coats of arms mingled with branches of leafwork on the keyhole plates, on bolts, and on sash-bolts. Quite often, the box took the form of a pediment from a Greek or Roman temple.

In the seventeenth and eighteenth centuries, lock mechanisms became even more complex. After being straight or ax-shaped in the Middle Ages and during the Renaissance, the bit of the key adopted the shapes of letters and numbers (fig. 13).

The use of half-turn bolts, and the pairing of them with deadbolts, dates from the seventeenth century. Renaissance styles return under Louis XIII, though heavier, while designs under Louis XIV took their themes from furniture. Even though they continued in the seventeenth century, repoussé and engraving techniques were slowly replaced by engraved copper and chiseled cast bronze, recalling gold-smith work. Finally, the second half of the eighteenth century witnessed the advent of chiseled cast iron enhanced with fire gilding.

A proliferation of rococo dolphins and cupids à la François Boucher (1703–1770) invaded the Louis XV period; in addition, a decorative knob for manipulating the bolt was often affixed to the lock. The cold, rigid design under Louis XVI reminds one of grillework.

Let us not forget *provostal* locks, with quite advanced mechanisms, designed to make them theft-proof. Their invention is attributed both to Duval and to Merlin, Parisian locksmiths at the end of the eighteenth century.

If you attempt to insert a fake key, the lock triggers two powerful springs that release two semi-circular clamps to trap the culprit; hence their name "provostal," as this lock takes the policeman's role (*prévot* in French) and stops the thief.

Merlin improved upon this system in 1782. Inserting a fake key triggered not only the clamps, but also a small bell fixed behind the fitting plate, as well as a powder charge from two small pistols.

Masterpiece locks, the chefs-d'oeuvre, were always executed in iron, with an antique-style façade. The mechanism is a marvel of precision: each component is decorated, and the fitting plate often covers a plate with refined carvings.

Wards were so tightly placed that the name "comb keys" was given to the keys designed to work them.

The closing on the lock box (figs. 22–25) was held by a clasp (Cl) fixed under the box's cover, which slid into two small keepers (K, K') hollowed on their tips. These keepers rotated on a stop pin (P) and were held in place by two springs (S) (figs. 22 and 23).

Turning the key pushed the tail (T) of the keeper (K). The other stem (K') moved away from the first with the help of an S that turned on a stop pin. When the keeper (K) was moved with the key, the S rolled, separating the keeper (K') and thereby freeing the clasp (Cl).

The bit of the key was pierced with several holes (A, B, C) that did not connect to each other or to the edge of the key (fig. 24). Because of this, the key could only make a partial rotation.

The semicircular wards, which corresponded to the holes, were held on parts (A^2, B^2, C^2) placed against each other.

The rake blades (D) were affixed to a vertical piece (D^2).

In addition, the key was piped; a pipe attached to the fitting plate was added to the aforementioned fittings.

Lock boxes with multiple bolts illustrate the ingenuity of master locksmiths.

Fig. 20 shows a locking system with twelve bolts.

When the cover was locked, the springs (S) pushed the bolts, which locked into an edge raised around the box that replaced the keeper.

Each bolt was held by two staples (A). A spring (S), connected to a notch in the bolt and held by a pin (P), pushed the bolt into the locking position (fig. 21).

To unlock, a key was inserted into the center of the cover; the keyhole usually had a secret cover. In addition, a false keyhole was cut into the façade on one side of the box.

A half-turn of the key pushed a notch (N) on a larger iron piece, the big bolt (B), which opened all of the bolts at the same time. When the big bolt moved, bars and rods moved right-angled or S-shaped levers that rotated on pins (P). By pivoting, these levers pulled the bolts and unlocked them from the ridge (fig. 20).

The movement of so many pieces did not happen without some friction. The box could become difficult to open because of this, and sometimes a small lever had to be put in the bow of the key to get it to turn.

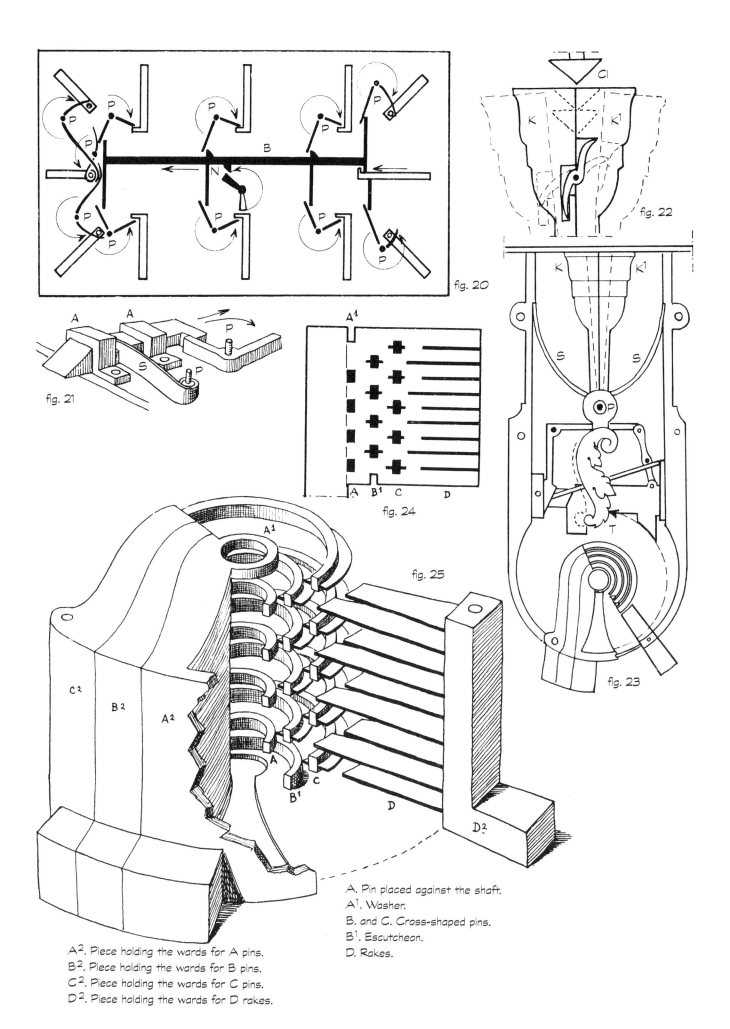

fig. 20

fig. 21

fig. 22

fig. 24

fig. 25

fig. 23

A². Piece holding the wards for A pins.
B². Piece holding the wards for B pins.
C². Piece holding the wards for C pins.
D². Piece holding the wards for D rakes.

A. Pin placed against the shaft.
A¹. Washer.
B. and C. Cross-shaped pins.
B¹. Escutcheon.
D. Rakes.

Latches

The latch, or *loquet* (from the old French *loc*), is a small lock, padlock, or clasp. Its English equivalent, lock, is still used today. The ordinary latch is an iron blade that secures a door, either by falling from its own weight or because a spring holds it down. Note the principal parts of a latch in fig. 1:

A. The latch, clapper, blade, or beam.
B. The holding staple, which prevents the latch from detaching from the door while still allowing it the necessary mobility.
C. The hinge pin.
D. The handle.
E. The keeper, affixed to the doorframe.

Even with a locking mechanism placed on the inside of the door, the latch can still be worked from outside with the help of various devices:

• The thumb latch

The thumb latch or thumb lock, for example, works with a lever pushed by the thumb (fig. 2). It is made up of a plate (A) and a handle (B) at least four fingers tall (C) and wide (D). The thumber (E) is moved with a slight downward push of the thumb. The latch is released from the hook with a small push of the thumb latch.

In a spring latch, a vertically moving rocker changes the rotation of a button or buckle, raising the clapper. You can see in fig. 3 the oval knob or handle (A), the plate (B), a square shaft (C), the rocker (D), the hook (E), and the spring (F).

• The vielle latch

This owes its name to its handle, comparable to that on the old musical instrument, the *vielle* (or hurdy-gurdy, in English), which moves the mechanism. This latch is shown in fig. 4. The plate (P) is recognizable; a pin (O), affixed to the inside, serves as the hinge for the bent lever (N), or vielle.

Also attached to the plate, a fitting (G) matches the key's escutcheon. The ensemble is protected by a cover (C) pierced with a hole that allows the end of the key to pass through.

• The cable latch

Already used by the Romans and Gallo-Romans, these locks were still in service in the eighteenth century under the name cable, pushrod, or Capuchin locks.

As can be seen in fig. 5, a key moves vertically against a small piece of metal (A) soldered to the latch arm (B), raising it and releasing it from the hook (C).

Security is maintained with a ward (D) connected to the plate, which matches the key's channels (E).

The whole mechanism is housed in an opening cut into the wood of the door. A back plate (F) protects the key and prevents it from entering too far; its curve matches that of the key. The latch is raised inside with a handle (G) riveted to the arm. The keyhole has a characteristic upside-down T shape.

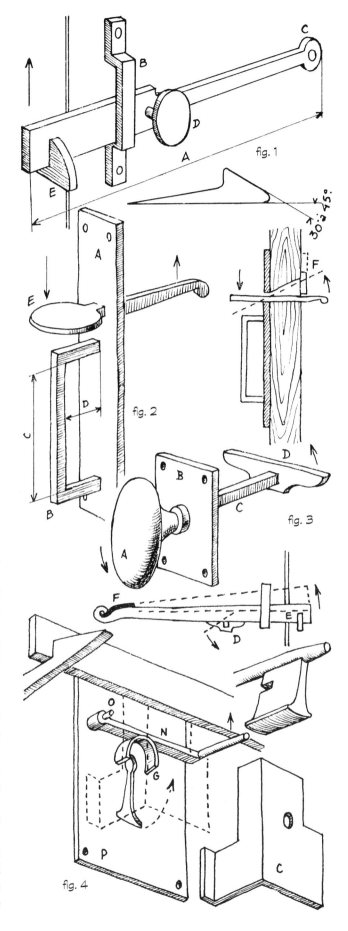

fig. 1

fig. 2

fig. 3

fig. 4

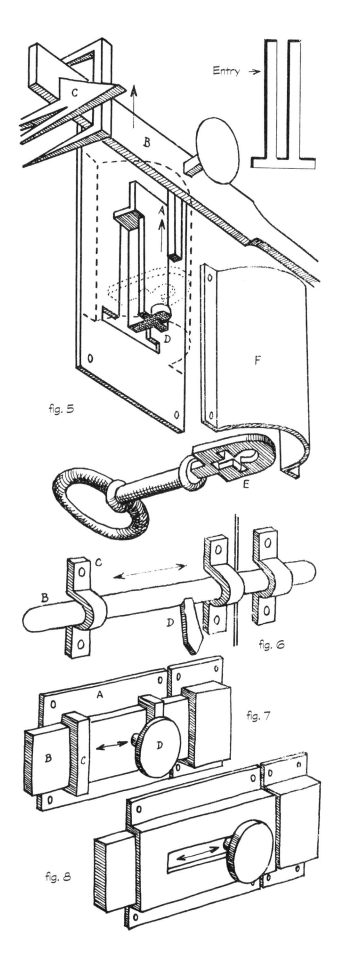

fig. 5

fig. 6

fig. 7

fig. 8

Bolts and Sash-bolts

The term *verrou* (bolt) comes from the Latin *veruculum*, small pin, and *veru*, pin; a small shield called the targe, used in the Middle Ages, gave its name to the *targette*, or sash-bolt.

The bolt is a piece of metal that moves transversally between two runners and locks a door or window by sliding into a keeper affixed to the doorframe.

The sash-bolt is a bolt with a flat shaft, sliding either in front of (fig. 7) or in back (fig. 8) of the plate; in the latter case, the bolt is said to be enclosed.

You can see in figs. 7 and 8 the plate (A), the bolt (B), and the runners or conduits (C), called bolt-staples. The knob, or handle (D), determines the bolts' range of movement.

History

The plate's design, executed in the Middle Ages in hammered iron and pierced in a ribbed pattern, makes way in the sixteenth century for orbe-voie patterning. The knobs, generally simple, as well as the end part of the bolt, cut in right angles, were sometimes enlivened with animal heads and, later, with human faces. This was the case with *coureils*, large bolts dating from the end of the fifteenth and sixteenth centuries. During this period, the plate was embellished with chimeras, branches, foliage, and coats of arms, treated in repoussé and chiseled metal.

In the seventeenth century, the plate was carved in simple patterns with a beveled edge.

In the eighteenth century, few decorative bolts were executed in iron.

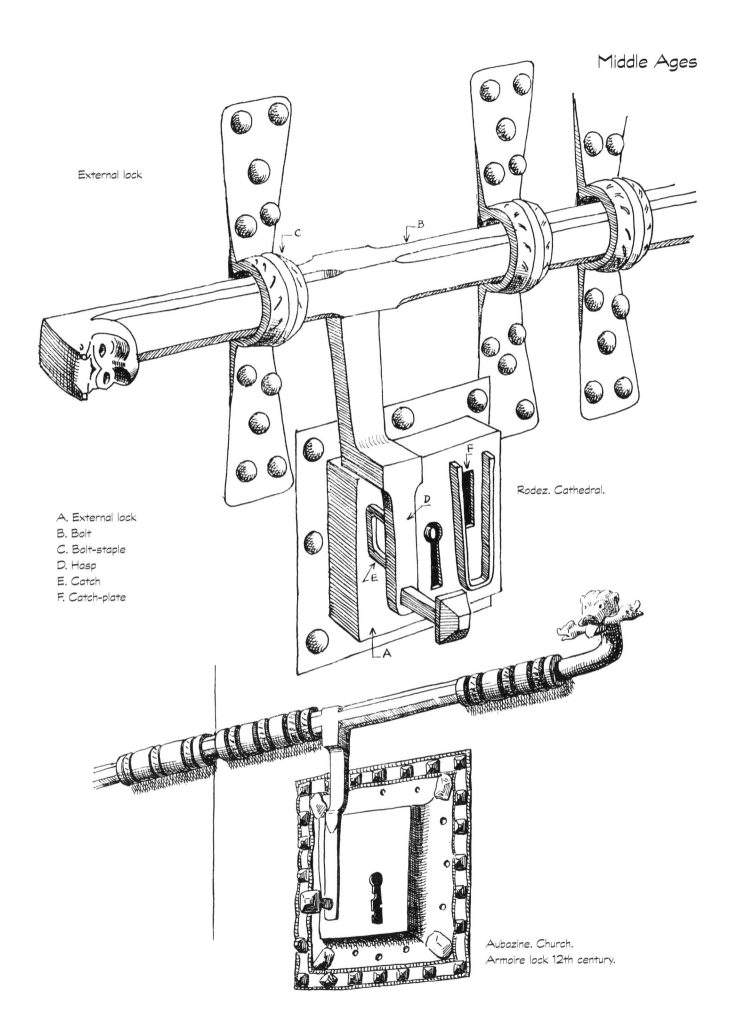

External lock

A. External lock
B. Bolt
C. Bolt-staple
D. Hasp
E. Catch
F. Catch-plate

Rodez. Cathedral.

Aubazine. Church.
Armoire lock 12th century.

Lock with hasp.
Pierced metal and orbe-voie design.

A. Hasp
B. Catch
C. Secret keyhole cover

15th century

Rouen.
Musée Le Secq des Tournelles.

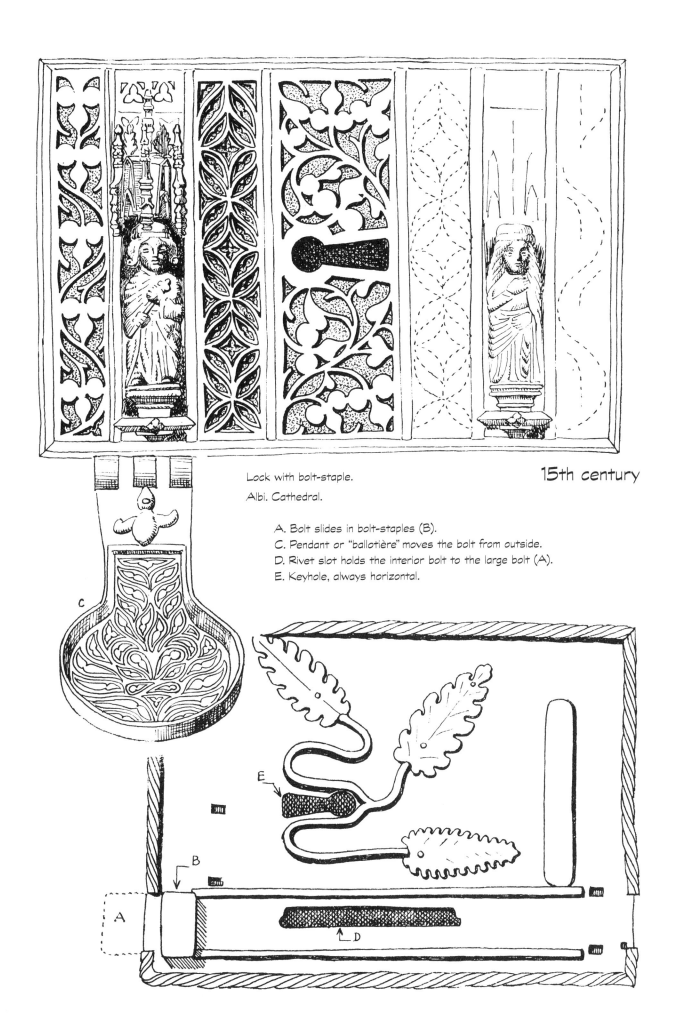

Lock with bolt-staple.

Albi. Cathedral.

A. Bolt slides in bolt-staples (B).
C. Pendant or "ballotière" moves the bolt from outside.
D. Rivet slot holds the interior bolt to the large bolt (A).
E. Keyhole, always horizontal.

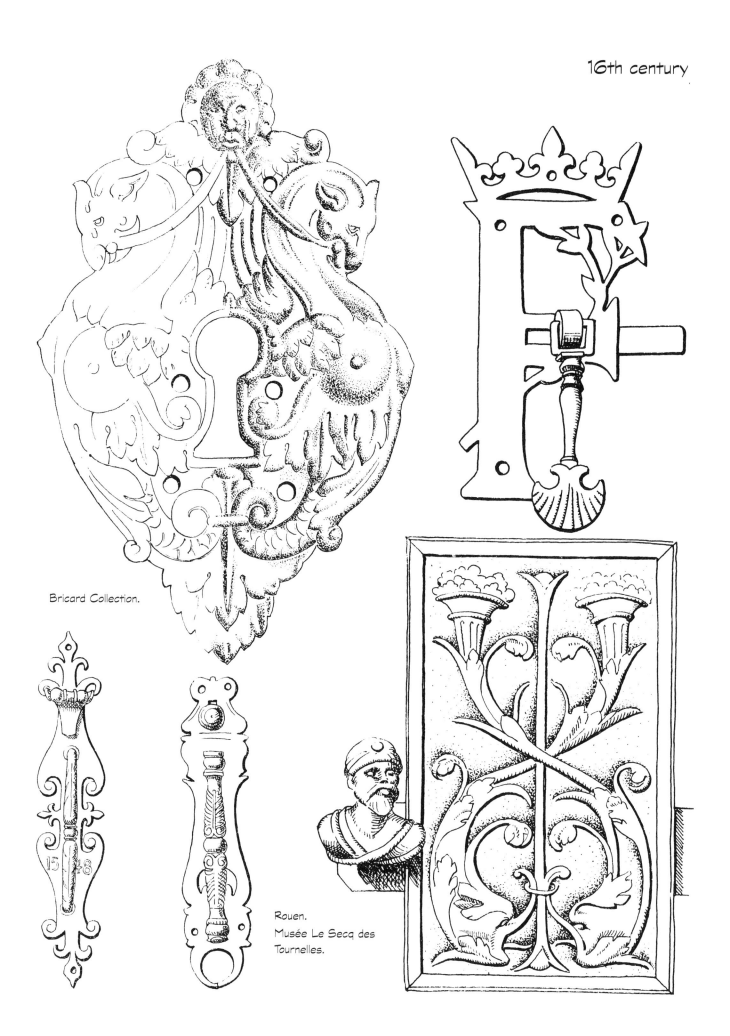

Bricard Collection.

Rouen.
Musée Le Secq des
Tournelles.

114

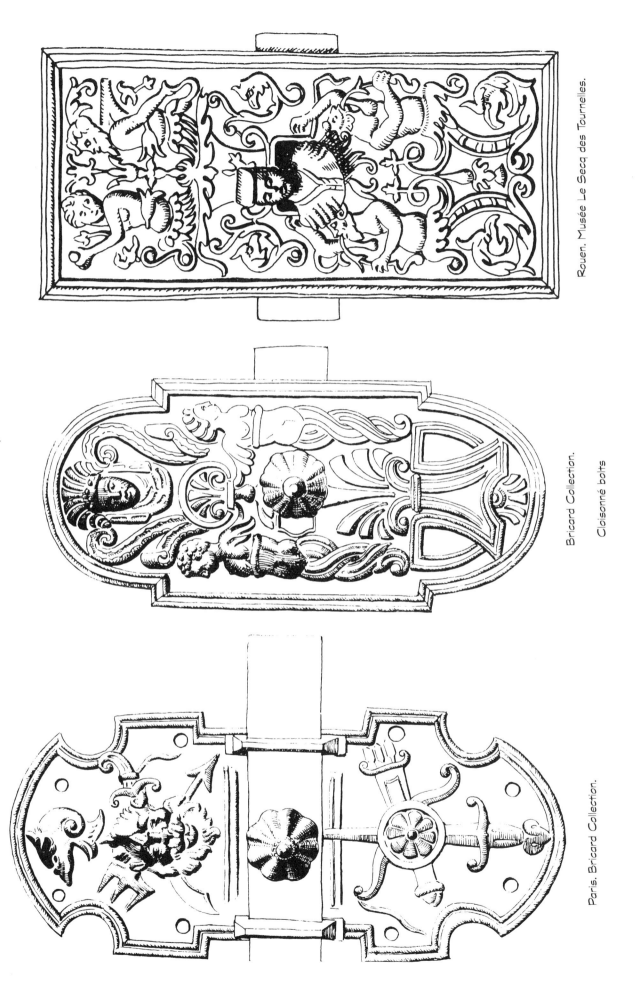

16th century

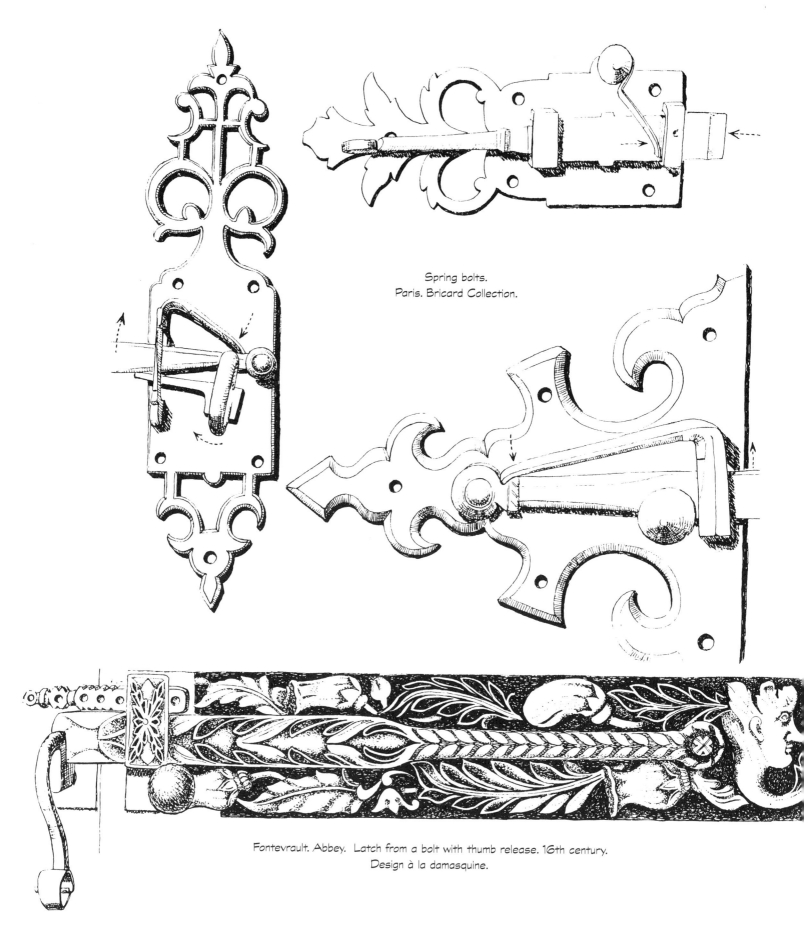

Spring bolts.
Paris. Bricard Collection.

Fontevrault. Abbey. Latch from a bolt with thumb release. 16th century.
Design à la damasquine.

116

Keys

The three main parts that make up a key are the bow, the shank, which is connected to the bow with a shoulder or collar, and the bit, which is affixed to the shank and pierced with openings called fittings, which correspond to those placed in the lock, or wards.

In the eighteenth century, the fittings had very specific names and were classed, depending on their notches, into five main types: there are the grooves on either the upper or lower side of the bit; the escutcheons on the end separating the bit from the shank; and the rakes, parallel notches cut into the front edge of the bit that are not as deep as the side grooves and form the key's teeth. When one of the raked notches, generally the middle one, extends more than the others in toward the shank, it is called a slot. When the slot is widened in the middle of the bit, or near the shank, this slit is called a channel.

The keys are arranged in the same way into categories based on the following characteristics:

1. The pin key has a solid shank that generally extends beyond the webbing. Pin keys may be used from either side of the lock. The fittings are symmetrical.
2. The piped key, with a hollow shank that slides onto a spindle or barrel affixed to the fitting plate. It only works from one side of the door. This is the case, for example, with armoire and bolt locks.
3. Pushrod, Capuchin, or cable keys, already in existence in Roman times, were still in used in the eighteenth century. They have no shank but a carved bit, thinned out near the handle. This was inserted horizontally in a T-shaped keyhole carved into the lock plate. The thinned part slid into the vertical slot and the bit moved a piece that in turn raised the bolt.

Symbolism

The key has always represented possession and, by extension, power.

Saint Peter is represented by the Keys of Heaven. The Keys of Saint Peter designate the spiritual power of the papacy. In the same fashion, the Power of Keys is the power to join or refuse—that is, to absolve or condemn—conferred upon the Apostles by Jesus, and the Keys of the Church's Treasures represent the ability to grant indulgences.

Chamberlain keys, distinguished marks of the chamberlain's dignity in the eighteenth century and only used on exceptional occasions to open a lock, were purely honorary.

By giving her husband a marriage key, a young wife granted him access to her bedroom.

Placing keys on someone's grave meant refusing his or her inheritance.

In early laws, the expression "to leave one's keys to justice" meant to cede one's belongings to one's creditors.

Finally, the keys of the city, which were used in the past to open and close the city's gates, remain a symbol of possession of the city.

There are a few iron specimens dating from the La Tène era. Roman keys with bronze bows and iron shanks and bits have also come down to us, as have Merovingian and Carolingian bronze keys, with their very large bows. But the iron key did not come into regular use until the twelfth century.

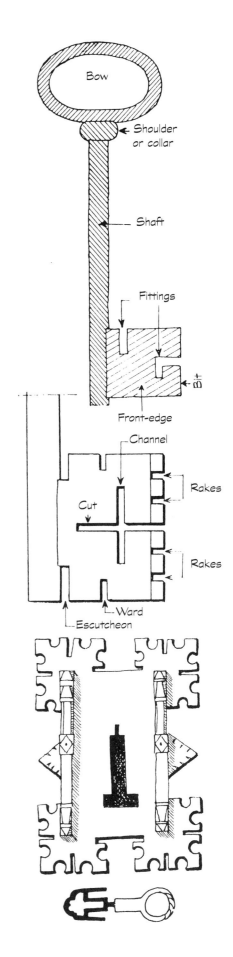

		BOW	COLLAR	SHAFT	BIT	FITTINGS
12th 13th		Small. Basic geometrical shapes.		Pin. Tipped with a long cone.	Very prominent, rectangular.	Very wide cuts.
13th 14th		Basic. Three- or four-leaf clover, then six or eight foils. Basic geometrical shapes.	Barely high-lighted in the 14th century.	Pin. Often tipped with a cone.	Prominent, thin, rectangular.	Wide cuts in right angles. Often staggered crosses in the 14th century.
15th Crown key		A cut crown tops a horizontal cylinder that forms a rosette, one- or two-sided, decorated with a cut design, most often in orbe-voie. Crown keys were originally masterpiece keys.	Parallelepiped. Engraved design.	Short. Piped, in general.	Rectangular.	Similar to preceding bits but more refined.
16th Masterpiece key		Truncated pyramid on a square base, cut in the latest style, topped with a person or molding. This pyramid stands on a cylinder decorated in the style of that period.	In general, elongated and decorated parallelepiped, or capital.	Very short and piped.	Front edge shaped like an ax.	Tight, refined cuts, in the shape of a cross near the shaft.
		In order to become a member of the locksmiths' guild, a candidate had to execute a masterpiece lock and key; the general form of the latter stayed the same from the 16th through 18th century.				
16th Henri II		Crisscross.	Capital or baluster.	Squat, piped in general.	Triangular, jutting front edge.	Right-angle cuts.
16th Key with chimeras		Leaning chimeras, birds, opposing dolphins. This last example was most in style in the 17th century.	Ionic or Corinthian capital. Sometimes moldings.	Stronger. Piped into a clover, heart, diamond, triangle, etc.	Same.	Fine, right-angled cuts.
		This style of décor continued into the 17th century, but with Henri IV engraving became more basic and the outside form more continuous. The bit and fittings made classifying keys simpler.				

BOW	COLLAR	SHAFT	BIT	FITTINGS		
Geometrical crisscrossing, "frogs' thighs," opposing dolphins holding a head or ball in their mouths, their bodies extend into leaves and their tails often end in doe's feet.	Ionic or Corinthian capital, sometimes moldings.	Thick. Often piped, round, square, or triangular with concave sides known as three-point fluting.	Protruding front edge.	Refined cuts in right, sharp, and wide angles.		Louis XIII
Opposing dolphins. Often branches of finely chiseled foliage, topped with a crown.	Molded.	Longer, often conical. Most often a pin key decorated with fluting; tipped with a ball.	Protruding or rectangular front edge.	Right-angled or widely curved cuts.		Louis XIV
Either floral design or monogram or coat of arms, or asymmetrical with a rococo pattern. Beginning with the second half of the 18th century, the design is sometimes enhanced with incrusted gold.	Molded or fluted.	Same.	Often shaped like letters or numbers.	Often widely curved cuts.		Louis XV
Floral or allegorical pattern.	Molded.	Molded or fluted.	Flat or shaped like a letter.	Generally in right angles.		Louis XVI

English keys. Imported starting at the end of the 17th century and mainly during the first quarter of the 18th century, English keys competed with French works, which were often executed in bronze. The bow, rather large, has various patterns and is finely chiseled.

Chamberlain keys. These keys, for the most part, were large and made of bronze that was chiseled and gilded. The bow was generally decorated with the owner's coat of arms. They were mostly in use in the 18th century.

Master keys. Made to open several locks, the master key has been in use since the end of the Middle Ages. The bit, with a very open layout, allowed them to pass between the lock's wards.

Two main types are worth mentioning. In the first, the master keys pivot on the bow, which is made of a series of cylinders.

In the second, two bits are affixed to the shaft's ends, with a small handle sliding into the unused bit to help with turning the key.

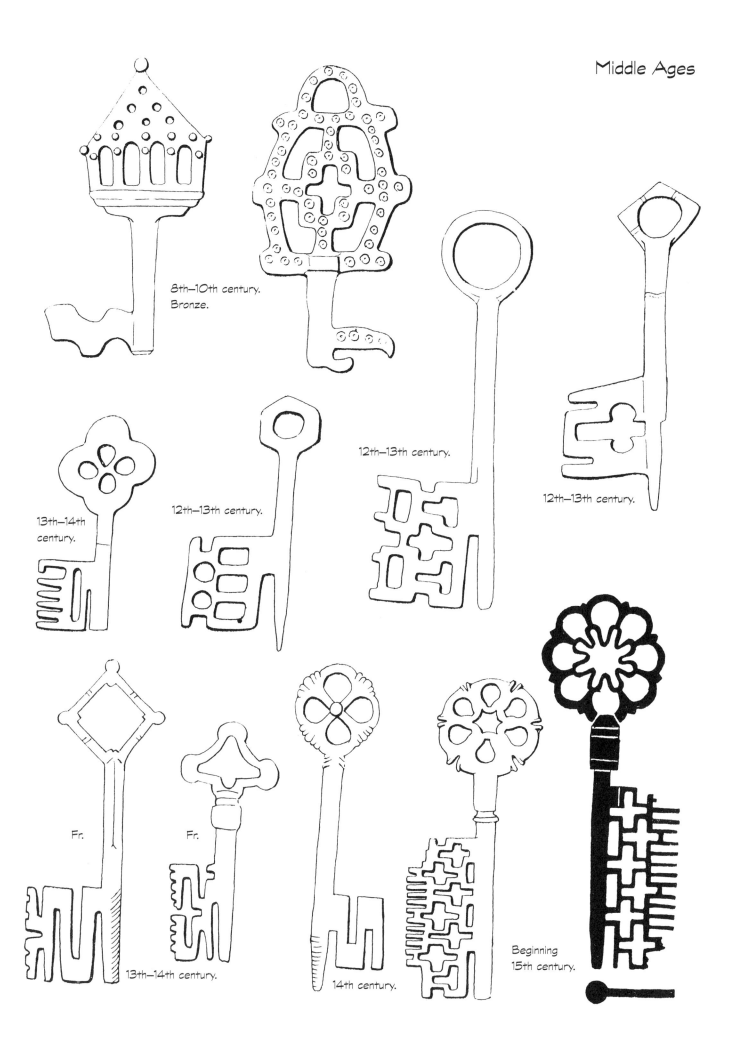

8th–10th century.
Bronze.

12th–13th century.

12th–13th century.

13th–14th
century.

12th–13th century.

Fr.

Fr.

13th–14th century.

14th century.

Beginning
15th century.

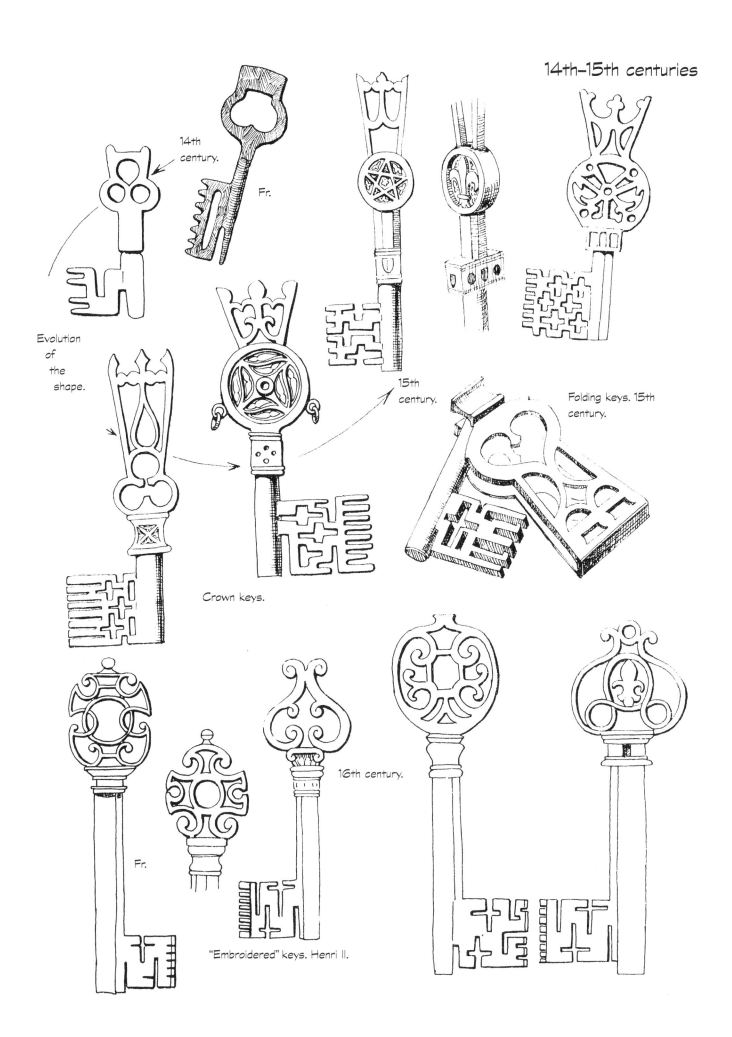

14th century.

Fr.

Evolution of the shape.

15th century.

Crown keys.

Folding keys. 15th century.

Fr.

16th century.

"Embroidered" keys. Henri II.

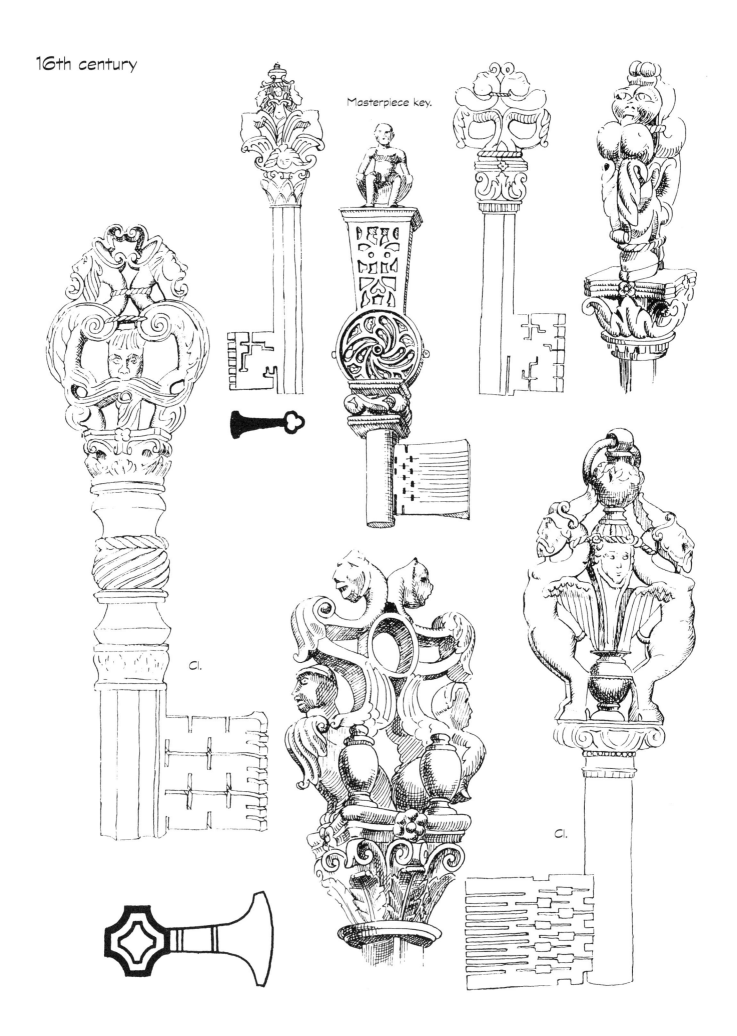

Masterpiece key.

cl.

cl.

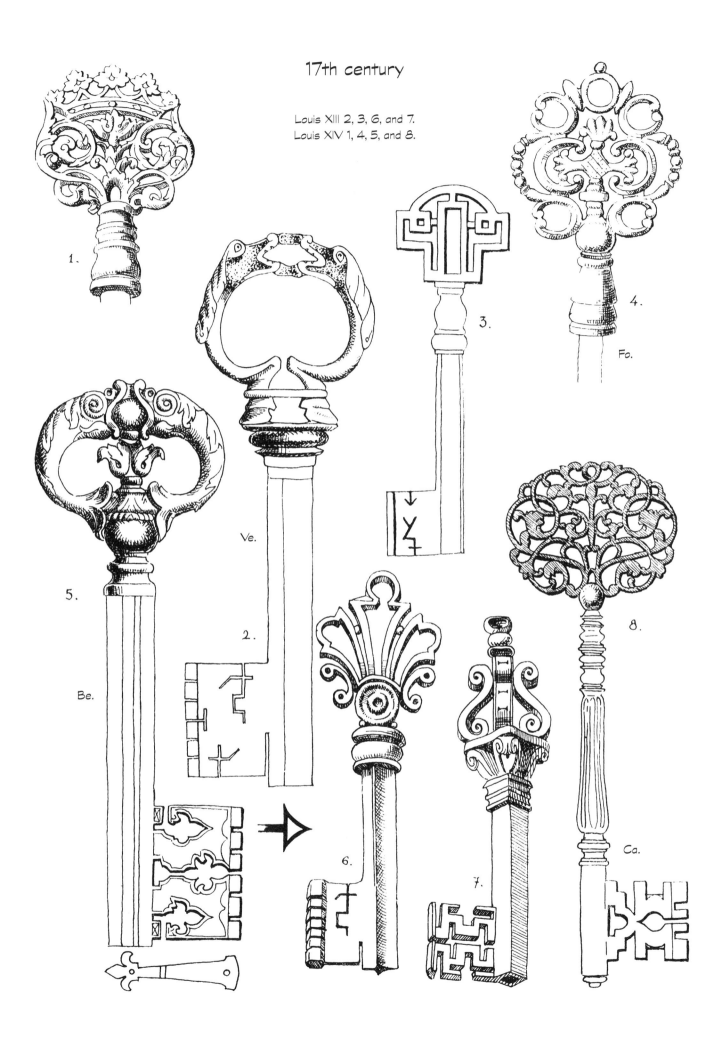

17th century

Louis XIII 2, 3, 6, and 7.
Louis XIV 1, 4, 5, and 8.

1.

2.

3.

4.

5.

6.

7.

8.

Ve.

Be.

Fo.

Ca.

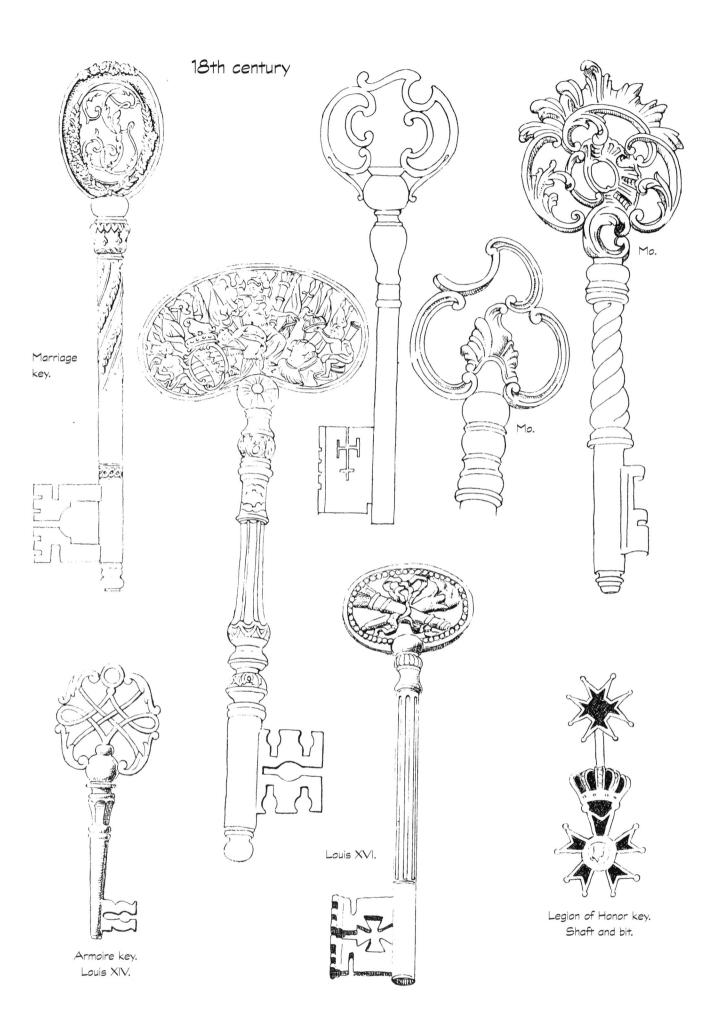

18th century

Marriage key.

Armoire key.
Louis XIV.

Louis XVI.

Mo.

Mo.

Legion of Honor key.
Shaft and bit.

124

18th–19th centuries

Chamberlain keys.

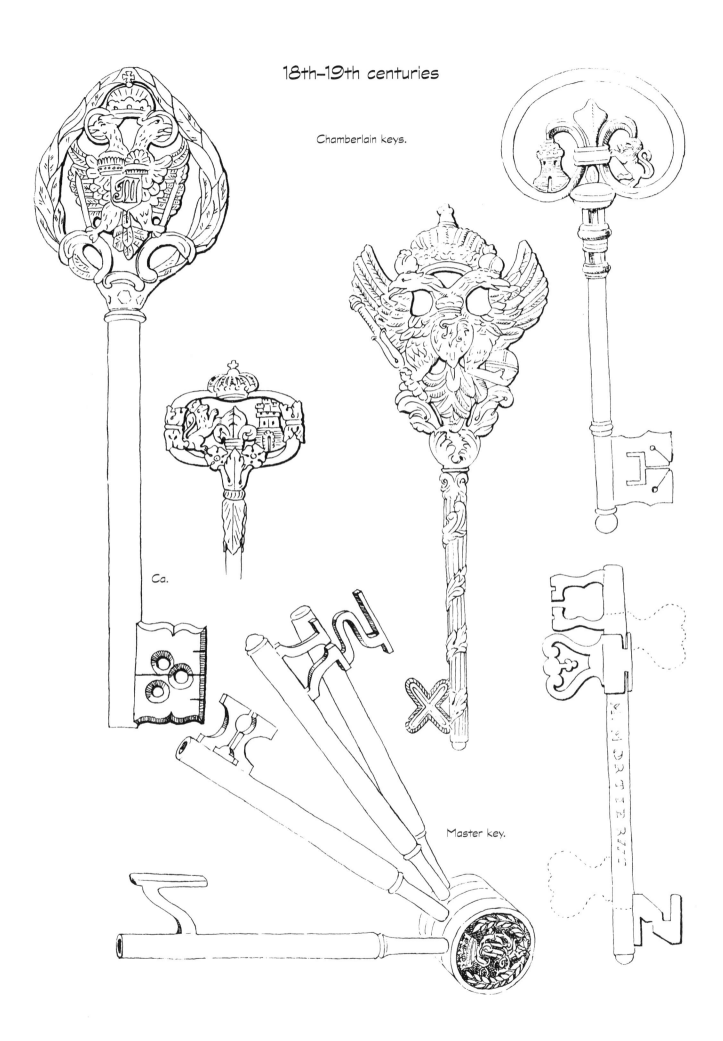

Ca.

Master key.

Bibliography

Agricola, Georgius [pseud. Georg Bauer]. *De Re Metallica.* Basel, 1556. Engravings illustrating mining and forging. English translation: H. C. and L. H. Hoover, London, 1912. Reprint, New York: Dover Publications, 1950.

D'Allemagne, Henry-René. *Les anciens maîtres serruriers et leurs meilleurs travaux*, vol. 2. Paris, 1943. Contains, besides numerous illustrations, a study on the corporations.
_____. *Histoire du luminaire*, Paris, 1891.
_____. *Catalogue du musée Le Secq des Tournelles*, vol. 2. Paris: 1924. (Reprint, *Decorative Antique Ironwork: A Pictorial Treasury.* Bibliography and translation of captions by Vera K. Ostoia. New York: Dover Publications, 1968.)

Bastien, A. P. *Le ferronnerie française contemporaine*. Paris: G. M. Perrin, 1961.

Bessoni, Jacobi. *Theatrum Instrumentorum et Machinarum.* Lyon: 1578. Illustrates human-driven tool machines.

Blanc, Louis. *Le fer forgé en France au XVIe et XVIIe siècles.* Paris and Brussels, 1928.
_____. *Le fer forgé en France, La Régence.* Paris and Brussels, 1930.
_____. *La ferronnerie à Bordeaux*. Paris: c. 1923. Sketches by the author.

Clouzot, Henri. *Le fer forgé*. Paris and Leipzig, 1953. Numerous documents on German and French ironwork.

Contet, F. *Ferronnerie ancienne*, vol. 7. Paris, 1925. Photographic documents of French ironwork.

Dechelette, Joseph. *Manuel d'archéologie préhistorique*. Paris, 1914. The origins of ironwork.

Frank, Edgar B. *Petite ferronnerie ancienne.* Paris, 1948. The author's own collection. English translation: *Old French Ironwork: The Craftsman and His Art.* Cambridge: Harvard University Press, 1950.

Frémont, Charles. *La Serrure, origine et evolution.* Paris, 1924. A study of the origins of the lock.

Gay, Victor. *Glossaire archéologique du Moyen Age et de la Renaissance*, vol. 2. Paris, 1887.

Haug, Hans. *Le ferronnerie strasbourgeoise au XVIIe et au XVIIIe siècle.* Paris and Strasbourg, 1933.

Jousse, Mathurin. *La fidelle ouverture de l'art du serrurier.* La Flèche, 1627. (Reprint, Paris: Librairie des Arts et Métiers, 1978.)

Lamour, Jean. *Recueil des ouvrages en serrurerie.* Nancy, 1767.

Loquet, Charles. *Essai sur la serrurerie à travers les âges.* Rouen, 1886. (Second edition, 1908.)

Magne, Lucien and Henri-Marcel. *Décor du métal: Le Fer.* Paris: 1929

Du Monceau, Duhamel, H. L. *Art du serrurier.* Paris, 1767. Text and engravings detail locksmithing techniques from the beginning of the eighteenth century.

Theophilus. *Diversarum Artium Schedula.* Paris, 1843. Treatise on medieval painting, glassmaking, and metalwork techniques. English translation: *Theophilus: On Diverse Arts.* (Translated from the Latin with introduction and notes by John G. Hawthorne and Cyril Stanley Smith. New York: Dover Publications, 1979.)

Viollet-le-Duc, E. *Dictionnaire raisonnné du Mobilier Français*, vol. 6. Paris, 1858.
_____. *Dictionnaire raisonné de l'architecture française de XIe au XVIe siècle*, vol. 10. Paris, 1854–1868.

The reader may also consult the portfolios of engravings at the Bibliothèque Nationale, the Bibliothèque des Arts Décoratifs, the Bibliothèque Doucet, the Bibliothèque des Beaux-Arts, and in the Lesoufaché Collection at the Ecole des Beaux-Arts in Paris.

Index